REDUNDANCY

Coping and Bouncing Back

REDUNDANCY

COPING AND BOUNCING BACK

JENNY WOOLF

PICCADILLY PRESS · LONDON

Phototypeset by Goodfellow & Egan, Cambridge
Printed and bound by WBC, Bridgend
for the publishers, Piccadilly Press Ltd.,
5 Castle Road, London NW1 8PR

A catalogue record for this book is available
from the British Library

ISBN 1–85340–194–3

Jenny Woolf is British and lives in North London with her husband
and two children. She is a freelance journalist, and has written for
most of the major national newspapers and magazines. This is her first
book.

AUTHOR AND PUBLISHER'S NOTE
*Although every effort has been made to ensure the book's accuracy at the
time of going to press, no legal responsibility can be taken for advice given.*

CONTENTS

DEDICATION

To Alan Grist, my father – with love and thanks for all
your help.

ACKNOWLEDGEMENTS

I would particularly like to thank Peter Smith of
HILL MARTIN plc for his advice regarding the
financial sections of the book.

Also, Bill Pitcher of CEDAR INTERNATIONAL,
Lewis Rushbrook of CEPEC, Rob Nathan of
CAREER CONSULTANTS, Zelda West Meads of
RELATE, GHN, COUTTS, the Institute of
Personnel Management, all the individuals whose
stories I quote in the book, and, of course, my
ever-supportive husband Tony.

And special thanks to Katherine, for all the cups of
tea.

INTRODUCTION

Jill Serota was planning to interview a new secretary when she arrived one June morning at the private hospital where she worked. Instead, she was called in to see the personnel manager. Suspecting nothing, she went to his office, to be told bluntly that the hospital group was losing money. It had decided to get rid of everyone at Jill's level, and would she please clear her desk right away.

'It was such a shock,' she recalls. *'I must have looked pretty terrible when I came out of his office. Nobody said anything to me as I packed up my desk – I wondered if they'd all known it was going to happen. I took the tube back to my flat, and just sat at my kitchen table for the rest of the morning like a zombie.'*

Being made redundant is always a shock, whether it comes as a total surprise, as in Jill's case, or after a long period of uncertainty, anxiety and rumours. Until the economic climate improves, more and more people will have to face up to the reality of redundancy.

That is the bad news. The good news is that redundancy can also be an opportunity. It can be a chance to move your career in new directions or alter an unsatisfactory lifestyle. It can provide a second chance to pursue ambitions that had got lost in the rat race.

1

Many people have seen their redundancy as a blessing in disguise. Simon Mason was made redundant from his job as account executive with a London advertising firm, and worked for a year afterwards as a gardening assistant. As he is single, without family responsibilities, he found the break from backbiting office politics a *'blessed relief'*.

He is now retraining as a social worker.

'I was forced to jump off the merry-go-round and think seriously about what I wanted to do,' he says. *'It sounds a bit corny, but doing manual work for a year helped me get in touch with myself again. Social work could hardly be more different from my past life, but it is more of an intellectual and social challenge than I have ever known.'*

The best way to cope with redundancy is to take as much control as you can. You can't prevent it, but you can try and turn it to your best advantage. You can be prepared for the effects it could have on both you and your family. You can plan your financial future, develop strategies for locating new jobs and techniques for obtaining them. Most important of all, you can learn from those who have built their lives after redundancy that losing your job does not remove your own worth.

This book will give you the information you need to help you do this.

Chapter One

REDUNDANCY IN THE AIR?

Warning – Job Hypochondria. Career Ownership.
General Precautions. Money Precautions.
Redundancy Insurance. Hanging On To Your Job.
Staying Friends.

WARNING – JOB HYPOCHONDRIA

Don't let a preoccupation with redundancy push you
into 'job hypochondria'. Symptoms include scanning
the papers for stories which suggest impending
redundancy in your field, discussing the subject
endlessly or stewing over it obsessively in private.

If you feel frightened at the idea of losing your job,
remember that many, many people have found that
even though they dreaded losing their jobs, and hated
actually being made redundant, they now feel that
their redundancy was a blessing in disguise.

Of course it is reasonable to try and protect your
future. By all means make changes in your lifestyle
you feel you can easily live with – such as reducing
expenditure. But don't try and solve problems that
haven't happened and may not happen. And definitely

3

don't let the prospect of redundancy take over to the
point where it stops you enjoying your life.

Philip's Story

'I'm sure there's nothing physically wrong with you,'
said the doctor, as Philip buttoned his shirt. Philip,
fifteen years as a manager in a national food
corporation, suspected that the doctor was right. His
sleeplessness, headaches and stomach aches had been
growing gradually worse since rumours had started
that his employer was planning mass redundancies.

It was a worrying situation and Philip was by nature
a worrier. Fortunately, he was also a fighter.

'The doctor gave me a tranquilliser prescription,' he
says. *'But I thought: I've got to face this. So I went home,
made myself a cup of coffee and sat down to think my
situation through logically. For the first time, instead of
pushing it out of mind, I thought about what I'd do if I
did lose my job. It seemed a terrifying idea. I felt as if I
was about to leap into the dark.*

*'I started thinking through the people I knew who had
lost their jobs, what had happened to them, and what
they'd done.*

*'I particularly remembered an auntie of mine who had
managed a little laundry in the 1950s. It closed down, and
she emigrated to Canada, and started a flower shop. In the
end she made a packet, by our standards. She had a really
nice house and a lovely car. Much better than if she'd
stayed in that laundry.*

*'I thought, well, I'll take a leaf out of her book. Do any
of us need a food company or a laundry to determine our*

whole future and peace of mind? I decided, this is MY life, and I can do what I want with it.'

Philip prepared himself for possible redundancy, and when the axe did fall he was ready. *'I won't lie, it was still awful when it happened. But I was prepared, and that helped me get my balance quite quickly. Now I'm training to be a surveyor. Nobody in my family ever did anything like that, so I'm going to be the first – I feel good about it.*

'If the job market hasn't picked up here by the time I qualify, I'm going to go and live abroad.

'I want a house designed by myself, and enough money. I want to live in the country and have a decent car. I'm not going to stop until I've got it. I can make what I want of my life.'

CAREER OWNERSHIP

Philip's discovery, though he didn't put a name to it, was the concept of career ownership, or taking responsibility for his own career pattern. It is still an unfamiliar notion to many people, but it has big advantages when it comes to coping with redundancy.

Company Man

Just a few years ago, the idea of career ownership was unknown. It was possible to join most big organisations and believe that you had a job for life.

REDUNDANCY

You were a Company Man (or, less often, a Company Woman).

The Fall Of Company Man
In recent years, even some of the most paternal (and apparently most secure) organisations have come under threat, while worsening economic conditions have caused many smaller businesses to collapse.

This has hastened Company Man's demise. But he had started to fade away even before the recession began.

Career Owner
Company Man is now being replaced by the Career Owner. The days have gone when your company took you on for life, promoted you when it was Buggins's turn and even decided where to relocate you.

In future more and more people will be thinking in terms of a series of careers with several different companies, perhaps with intervals of retraining or updating.

This doesn't suit everyone, of course, particularly those who want a quiet and regular life. But for most others the concept of career ownership is a revelation. It means their lives do not need to be made miserable by the threat of redundancy. Redundancy becomes a blip on the career pattern, a problem to be solved, rather than a total catastrophe.

REDUNDANCY IN THE AIR?

Early Retirement?
If you are getting on, or are perhaps in poor health, you might be tempted to suggest to your employers that you take early retirement. This is not at all a good idea. Do not volunteer for early retirement of your own accord or you will risk losing your redundancy pay. The situation will be quite different if your employer *asks* you to volunteer for early retirement. In that case you would be entitled to a payment.

Don't Take The Initiative To Go
The same thing applies if you volunteer to leave without being asked to. If you decide to leave your job of your own accord, you can't expect redundancy pay, even if the company is in difficulties and the prospects don't look bright for you.

GENERAL PRECAUTIONS

The stigma which was once attached – unfairly – to redundancy is beginning to disappear as organisations close down whole branch offices or dispense with entire layers of management. Anyone made redundant now is in excellent company, and many people have coped with redundancy several times and still done well. If you feel that redundancy is a possibility, then there are certain sensible precautions you can take without going to too much trouble.

REDUNDANCY

Find Your Contract Of Employment

Perhaps you shoved your employment contract in a
drawer years ago and haven't looked at it since. Dig it
out and read it. What period of notice does it give you?
What redundancy pay would you be entitled to? You
will be in a better position to negotiate your severance
package if you know what it says, or even where it is.
So refresh your memory *now*.

You might find that your contract contains a few
surprises – good or bad. If you spot these while you are
still employed, you'll have the chance to think about
them in an unpressurised way and decide how best
you'd tackle any problems or exploit any advantages
which present themselves.

Search Through The Files

One of the best ways of getting another job is
networking – putting the word around that you're
seeking work – and the more people you can network
with, the better. However, if you have to clear your
desk in a hurry, you may not get the chance to collect
the details you need.

One dull day, go through the files and pull out the
names and details of every single person you think you
might find useful if you leave your job. If you don't
have a good memory for personal detail, take copies
of as much information on each person as you need.
(Don't, of course, remove anything confidential or
which belongs to your employer.) You should end
up with a nice little file of contacts and background
information. Update it regularly.

8

REDUNDANCY IN THE AIR?

This strategy helped executive Ralph Andrews who was told he was no longer needed one February morning.

'As it happened, I'd talked to a colleague in the States who said he'd collected information from the office files about everyone who could possibly be useful to him in the future,' he says. *'I knew which way the wind was blowing for me, so I did the same. They didn't give me much time to pack up and so I was damn glad to have the stuff when I began looking for another job.'*

Company Benefits

Does your company offer benefits like, for instance, private health care? If so, use them to the full. Go on, get that checkup. Check too to see whether the company will continue your cover if you continue paying premiums until the membership year has elapsed.

Check whether you will be able to keep certain benefits – for instance, some companies offer death-in-service or injury insurance protection. Should you make a note to consider new arrangements?

Contingency Plan

Some people find it useful to sit down and write out – even cost out – a plan of how they could cope in the first few weeks if they were suddenly made redundant. It has the advantage of suggesting a definite routine to follow during a period when you might be too shocked to think clearly or do anything.

MONEY PRECAUTIONS

Once you start looking at your finances you'll probably realise that you can do several things that will benefit you even if you're never made redundant.

Beware Debt
Don't take out any big loans if you're concerned about your job. Make up your mind to do without your new kitchen for a while.

Exceptions to this rule are real essentials, like dry rot repairs or a replacement car if you live in the country and your old car has given up. You should see to this kind of thing while you are still employed and able to get a loan or credit. Consider taking out redundancy insurance on the loan.

Trim Spending Habits
It is fairly painless to trim your spending habits. You can put the money you save into a building society or instant access regular savings scheme. Going through your bank statements could reveal to you, as it did to

REDUNDANCY IN THE AIR?

PR consultant Anna Frear, that you have gradually slid into bad financial habits without realising.

'I'd always thought I was quite economical,' she says. *'My local supermarket lets you draw cash on Switch when you pay for the groceries. I go in most evenings to buy my supper and often I'd draw a few pounds for spending money. When I bought clothes and larger items, I always paid for them with Visa. I kept tabs on Switch, Visa and my bank balance, but when I sat down and actually totalled up what I spent every month I was amazed. It was a fortune.'*

Anna decided to reduce her spending by 10 per cent. She calculated how much she spent on clothes, food and sundries per week, put her cards away and drew each week's money out in cash. She is still baffled by the fact that although she is now spending 10 per cent less she doesn't notice it. *'I guess it's some kind of psychological thing. I hesitate more about handing over real money than I do about waving plastic,'* she says. *'Also, because I don't like carrying large amounts of cash I usually leave some of my money at home. That's stopped a lot of impulse buying – and I obviously don't want most of the stuff either, because I can never be bothered to go out and get it later when I've got the cash.'*

Special Fund
Put the money you save in a special building society account as a 'special fund'. Earmark the fund to tide you over some of the initial financial pains of losing your job.

Outplacement agencies confirm that most of their

clients get another job in a few months. So, if you lose your job, you'll probably get another one before too long. Meanwhile, what about buying Christmas presents, renewing your prized golf club membership or paying for your child's ballet lessons – all strictly inessential but somehow important things?

This is where your fund will come in. It won't solve your long term problems but it could help cushion the emotional blow for a while – hopefully till you get another job.

REDUNDANCY INSURANCE

Redundancy Insurance On Loans

You can get unemployment insurance on many loans and mortgages, though usually it's only available when you take the loan out. Premiums used to be low, but they are rising as insurers suddenly realise they're being hit for more and more claims. More and more mortgage companies, however, are requiring such insurance before they grant mortgages.

Income Protection

Income protection insurance for the unemployed is not very common. As the unemployment statistics get worse, the already-high premiums get higher, and insurers get less keen to quote.

REDUNDANCY IN THE AIR?

Income protection insurance of this type isn't wholeheartedly recommended by many experts. *'Where do you draw the line insuring against things?'* asks one. Another says: *'It depends if you are the kind of person who gets peace of mind from being heavily insured no matter what the cost.'*

Read Your Policy
Most insurers only pay out if you actually sign on, but you may not wish to do this for various reasons. Most only pay up if you have been out of work for a certain period and usually only if you become redundant within a specified time of taking it out.

HANGING ON TO YOUR JOB

Hanging on to your job has not been given its own chapter for the simple reason that in a bad recession most job losses occur for reasons which have little to do with any individual's performance. You could be the most organised person in the world, as clever as Einstein and as helpful as Milly-Molly-Mandy, but that would not necessarily stop your company from folding up with you in it.

However, sometimes you can do things which could make the boss choose to let someone else go instead of you.

REDUNDANCY

Cut Costs
The most obvious thing you can do to make yourself useful is to find new ways of cutting costs and subtly making sure everybody important knows about this. Perhaps you can suggest ways of cutting down contract staff, or completing a project more cheaply.

Strengthen Your Own Position
You could also concentrate on stengthening your position within your company. If your department's future looks shaky, perhaps you could transfer to a similar job in a rather healthier division. You should also make a special effort to forge cordial links with everyone who might be useful. (But be unobtrusive. Draw the line, for instance, at sending the managing director a lavish bouquet on his birthday.)

Get Your Skills Up To Scratch
You may want to do more if you feel that your own efforts really could help you keep your job. You can polish up and maintain your job skills. Read some of the books on job effectiveness to find out what the experts say you should do to achieve maximum effectiveness in your type of work. Compare this with how you think you are actually handling the job and identify what seem to be your weakest points. Then, in conjunction with the book, decide how you can improve them.

A book, *How to Survive and Prosper in a Recession*,

contains a chapter on keeping your job in bad times. Much of it is concerned with advancing your career, but it is also worth reading in order to get a general insight into the super-survivor approach to life.

Courses

Your employer probably won't be offering to pay for skills updating courses. Do you want to pay for a part-time course yourself? If you get made redundant it could be useful. However, some employers can be persuaded to pay the fees for skills updating courses as part of a severance package, so don't rush into paying for something if you may have the chance of getting it free.

Pierrot Not Required

Try and avoid pathos. Even if you sincerely believe that you, of all people, deserve to be kept in the company, resist the temptation to plead openly for your job. If they were going to keep you anyway, it will make you look silly, and if your boss has decided you must go, he or she won't have a change of heart just because you are down there on bended knees. The embarrassment of such a situation could even force your employers to reject you more harshly than they would otherwise have done.

Likewise, if you think an announcement is in the air, don't try and pre-empt it by asking colleagues to put in a word for you or help you avoid the axe. They will probably be worried about their own jobs, and may not be able to do as much for you as you think they can.

If you plead for help and then get fired anyway, it will make you look pathetic. This will embarrass everyone – which could make it harder for you to embark on successful networking with them in the future.

STAYING FRIENDS

The people you leave behind you will not disappear off the face of the earth. One day, you may meet again. They could turn up – perhaps years later – in a position where they can do you good or harm.

'One of the main lessons I have learned is to remain on good terms with the people I've left behind,' says Bill, who spent most of his working life in the water industry. *'I changed jobs several times and tended to leave on bad terms, because I would detach myself mentally from the job before leaving. When I was made redundant I purposely remained on good terms with everyone.'*

Chapter Two

BARGAINING

Never Let Them See You Sweat. Negotiations.
Rights And Duties.

Anyone who has just been made redundant will
probably be in quite a state of shock, and definitely not
in the best mental state for negotiating.

*'I hardly remember anything of that day.' 'I felt like a
zombie.' 'I couldn't believe it.' 'My flatmate said I was as
white as a sheet.'*

If you're still employed and are worried you may
lose your job, then concentrate on the early part of this
chapter, which will help you prepare yourself for
dealing with any negotiations.

If you've already been made redundant and haven't
done some of the things you should have done, don't
blame yourself. There will probably still be things you
can do to improve matters. Knowing your options is
half the battle, and the latter part of the chapter
focuses on these.

NEVER LET THEM SEE YOU SWEAT

Leave Them Standing If You Have To

You are likely to be in a state of shock immediately after learning the news. So just remember this: If you don't feel you can cope with negotiating your severance terms calmly, leave without agreeing anything, and come back when you can cope.

This may only be a matter of excusing yourself and disappearing to the washroom for a few moments. Or, if you have a friend whom you can trust, you may be able to spend a few moments with them and ask them to 'talk you down'. But whatever you do, don't rush into signing anything until you can cope.

Always let them do the talking. All you need to say is that you'll think about it. If they give you anything in writing, take it away with you. You don't need to read it there and then.

You Are Number One

If your employer doesn't like this, it's too bad. You don't want to be rude, but he or she must just wait until you can do justice to considering the terms on which you will be leaving.

You are not going to rush off, pack a suitcase and disappear forever. You are going to acknowledge that you are making very important decisions, and if you don't treat yourself like Number One at this stage, nobody else will.

BARGAINING

Keep Your Dignity

Laura was an executive in a manufacturing company. Her boss began to have an affair with Laura's colleague, Mandy. When the business began to do badly, Laura, not Mandy, was the one who was asked to leave. Laura believed, with justification, that she was being singled out unfairly. As she had just bought a flat with a huge mortgage, she was both angry and frightened when she confronted her boss.

'Everything was boiling inside me. I'd been with the firm longer than Mandy, and I was more competent than her. I had a mortgage, she had a husband to support her. He'd behaved very badly indeed – his wife was pregnant and he was carrying on with Mandy and firing me. Oh, I really wanted to say all kinds of awful things – dreadful things. But I didn't say a word of it. I was icy cool. I've never exerted such self control. And I managed to negotiate a better leaving package than I was strictly entitled to, because he felt guilty.'

Keeping your dignity will help you more than getting hysterical, making threats, being sarcastic or causing a major scene will. Even if you would cheerfully consign your employers to outer space forever, you will do yourself more good by staying on civil terms with them, at least initially, and at least on the surface. As Laura said: *'One day, I'll get my own back – if I still care.'*

M'Lud . . .

The idea of taking legal action may flit through your mind if you are particularly angry. By all means take legal advice if you think you need it, but if you are tempted to go through with a court case consider firstly that cast iron cases are few and far between, and secondly, consider what impression you will make on potential future employers if you go to the law. Will they queue up to hire someone who is litigious?

In any event, do not threaten your employer with legal action unless you are 100 per cent sure of your ground. And it will probably be helpful if you discuss your problem with your union or professional body.

In two years' time, your feelings will probably be very different – but what happens now could still be affecting your life.

You Have Some Advantages

Whether you find yourself negotiating with your superior or with the personnel department, remember that the dice are not all loaded on their side. You will have certain things going for you.

The Worst Job In The World

You can be pretty sure that the individual making you redundant will be feeling awful too. If he or she is a kindly soul, or knows you well, they will be heartbroken (perhaps behind a calm exterior) at your plight. If they have a heart of stone, they'll be hoping you won't cause trouble, threaten anyone or cause a scene. Either way, they will do everything to keep up a

BARGAINING

calm, reasonable but unemotional front and will be
dying to get you out of there and the whole business
concluded as quickly as possible. That is your
employers' main weakness. *You* don't want to dispose
of the problem of yourself as quickly as they do.

Walk Tall

Most people who have been made redundant feel
rejected and unwanted, and need some time to pick
themselves up. If rejection makes you want to run
away and hide, remind yourself that you'll certainly
feel differently in a while. Before long, your sense of
your own worth will creep back, and you really will
recover your equilibrium. Meanwhile, hold back the
tears and stand up for a fair deal even if you'd really
like nothing better at the moment than to jump off the
top of Canary Wharf.

Edward, a chartered engineer, had been with the
same firm for 36 years. They gave him a warning of
redundancy and a long period of notice, most of
which, he said, he spent '*crying inside. But by the time I
actually came to leave, I'd stopped feeling sad and had
started to feel quite cross with the firm. I decided they'd
treated me rather badly after all my years of loyalty. So I
marched in and suggested politely that they improved
various aspects of my severance package. At first they said
no, but I persisted. Then to my surprise they agreed. I was
thrilled. I hadn't been rude, you know, but I think it
surprised them that I stood up for myself and just wasn't
prepared to play the "dear old Edward" role any more.*"

21

Use Your Skills

Do not hesitate to capitalise on your talents. If you have a sales background, now is the time to use your hard-won negotiating skills. If you are keen on sports, compare this event to a big race or an important match, prepare yourself and give it all you've got. If you have an analytical mind, now is the time to get it into gear. Keep control of yourself and your negotiations.

Calming Measures

You may or may not be keen on relaxation exercises, but if you have the chance to prepare for your settlement interview beforehand, then relaxation could help you achieve a calm state of mind. An effective relaxation technique is given at the end of Chapter 5.

Oafs

Unfortunately, sheer insensitivity is something you may have to deal with when you become redundant. You should prepare yourself for the possibility that you may have to face an oaf somewhere along the line. Some people just don't seem to have any social skills. Ian, a middle manager, still bristles at the memory of his personnel manager's crassness. *'He treated me with what felt like contempt and never even thanked me for all my hard work,'* he says. *'That idiot had an emotional age of 14 years. I coped by telling myself that he was obviously lousy and rotten at his job, which he was.'*

NEGOTIATIONS

Union
If you can, contact your union, trade or professional association to see if they have any advice or recommendations for members who are being made redundant.

Know Your Rights
Chapter 1 dealt with preparing for possible redundancy. It suggested taking a look at your contract of employment. This will tell you exactly what you are entitled to and how much notice you can expect. If you are fully aware of what your contract contains, you will have some perspective on any deal your employer offers, and might even be able to negotiate for more. And at the end of this chapter is a section on employers' duties and employees' rights.

If The Business Has Closed
If the business you worked for has gone into liquidation, you are unlikely to get more than the state redundancy payments. However, your pension fund should still be secure. If the business has been sold to someone else, you may have been transferred automatically to work for the new owner, and your entitlements will obviously be different. If you are in this position, and are suspicious that you are not getting your entitlements, consult your union and take

23

brief legal advice if you can. Never rush into litigation, but if you have the law on your side it will certainly strengthen your negotiating position.

Retraining

Some companies offer their redundant staff extra training to help them get another job. If they mention it, make sure you tie up all the details, including exactly how it is to be paid for.

Consultancy

If you think you might wish to offer your services on a freelance basis after you have left the company, mention this at the termination interview. (See Chapter 11 for more about consultancy.)

Explain What You Need

The person you are negotiating with probably won't have thought much about specific difficulties you might face. You should point them out, and indicate ways in which the company could make your adjustment to a new life easier. Sometimes it won't cost them a lot or be much trouble to them – they just need to be told.

BARGAINING

How Could They Help?
Mike worked in Bath and he and his family lived in a tiny village with no public transport. Mike could have managed by using his wife's car, but this would have been highly inconvenient for them both. When he explained this, his company agreed to let him have a further six months' free use of his company car after he left, and when that time was up they decided to sell it to him at a hefty discount.

Reference
Don't forget to discuss the matter of a reference.

The Power Of The Pen
It sounds obvious, but don't rely on anything until you have it in writing. Even if you have been on excellent terms with your employer until now, you must safeguard yourself by getting every single thing down on paper and signed. Make sure that the facts and figures that you have agreed are correct.

Taking Early Retirement
If you are taking early retirement then you should have checked how your pension will be affected. If not, do so before you agree to sign anything. Depending on your age, and what the scheme provides, the penalties can be surprisingly high. It is safest to ask if you can

speak with the company's pensions adviser or take independent advice, but you could also research the subject thoroughly yourself, perhaps with the help of the TUC. For more about this, see Chapter 3, *Financial Matters*, Chapter 4 *Your Redundancy Payoff And Pension*, and the further information section at the end of the book.

RIGHTS AND DUTIES

You have certain rights under the law, and employers must fulfil certain duties. The following is a simplified version of these. Your local Citizen's Advice Bureau can offer advice and your Jobcentre should be able to offer you booklets which go into more detail if you need it.

Employers' Duties
Employers must take all reasonable steps – like reducing overtime or laying off contract workers – to minimise redundancies. They should also redeploy staff or offer retraining if appropriate. Employers must also consult staff and unions about impending redundancies, state why the redundancies are necessary, how many workers will be affected and how they propose to choose which staff to lose. Their criteria for selection must be 'fair and reasonable' involving factors like length of service, conduct, experience, age and attendance record.

BARGAINING

Notice
You may be asked to accept pay in lieu of notice which
will have the added benefit of being tax free. If this
happens you may find that your redundancy insurance
will not pay out until your notice period has expired.
At the time of writing a case is going to appeal on this.

Don't Jump The Gun
You may be extremely keen to leave your job, or even
have another job fixed up, but if you think redundancy
is imminent, don't be tempted to leave of your own
accord (this includes volunteering for early
retirement). Tim was a warehouse manager whose
employer invited him to leave of his own accord to
'avoid the stigma of redundancy'. Tim was cool
enough to say no. He had once worked in a social
security office and knew that if he lost that 'redundant'
label he would lose many benefits too.

Benefit is also lost if you are made redundant but
leave before your redundancy takes effect. However, if
you stick out your notice (whether your redundancy
was voluntary or otherwise) to the bitter end, you will
not lose any benefit.

Jobseeking Time Off
Your employer ought to allow you paid time off to seek
another job if you have worked for the company for
more than two years and have been made redundant.

REDUNDANCY

Holidays
Your employer should pay you for any annual holiday entitlements you haven't taken. You could also ask for additional time off for interviews.

Alternative Employment
At present many employers are having to lose people they wish could stay in their present jobs, so they may not be able to offer you alternative paid employment within the company.

   If they do offer you comparable alternative employment and you refuse it, you will lose your entitlement to redundancy pay unless the job is obviously totally unsuitable for you. If you accept the alternative employment, you'll be allowed a month to try it out. If it turned out to be unsuitable, you would then be entitled to become redundant and keep your entitlements.

Notice Period – Don't Lose Your Rights
If you get another job during your period of notice, be sure that your old employers agree to let you go without your redundancy payments being affected. If they choose to be difficult you could lose your redundancy entitlement.

Now Deal With The Feelings

Even though it is vital to overcome your feelings when you're trying to negotiate, don't box them away afterwards. They need to be worked through and come to terms with. Chapter 4 deals with coping with and working through your feelings.

Chapter Three

FINANCIAL MATTERS

*First Things First. State Benefits. State
Redundancy Payments. Balancing The Budget.*

FIRST THINGS FIRST

It has been said that an economist is someone who tells
you what to do with your money after you have done
something else with it. So if you haven't had the
chance to prepare for redundancy, your first reaction
may be to deny the money problem and try and carry
on just as before.

Don't. Pretending that nothing has changed is a
burden all of its own, as Londoners David and Jeanne
Schultz discovered. When David, a very highly paid
executive, was ousted in a merger, the couple decided
not to change their opulent lifestyle in any significant
way. Instead, they spent freely from the large lump
sum payment David received *'supposedly to boost our
morale'* says Jeanne.

As the months went on, no suitable opportunities
appeared for David. Mortified at what he felt was his
failure, and secretly terrified of financial catastrophe,

he found solace in lavish socialising and a girlfriend. Jeanne felt angry and neglected. *'While David was running off to some young girl he thought would admire him, I was worrying about the family's future. Money goes horrifyingly fast when you have no income, and we were just squandering it,'* she recalls. *'I read newspaper stories about people who had lifestyles rather like ours coming to grief, and I started wondering: "What if he never gets another job? He is 50, after all."'*

Fortunately David got another high-powered job fairly soon. He and Jeanne have patched their marriage up, but Jeanne is determined that if he ever loses his job again she will insist on setting a sensible budget from the start. *'I can't change his nature, but although I'm not at all a bossy person I think I would insist that we got the money under control and didn't live in cloud cuckoo land.'*

Whether your salary has been high or low, the sooner you get full control of your finances, the more money you'll have to play with.

'Winning The Pools'

You may well get a lump sum to compensate you for being made redundant. This may be a couple of thousand pounds, or it may be a great deal more. Resist the temptation to rush into using it for whatever catches your fancy. You must stop and think what to do before you rashly leap into paying off your mortgage or buying yourself some treats. If you are used to getting a regular salary, then suddenly finding yourself with a lump sum might feel a little bit like winning the pools. It seems tempting to have a nice holiday, or take a comfortable couple of months off before you start looking for another job.

But remember that you have been thrown into an unfamiliar financial situation. While you can't just leap into it and handle it perfectly right away, you must avoid seeing your lump sum as a windfall. Take some time to consider your situation, read this chapter carefully and take proper financial advice if you think you need it.

The pools companies know that winners can be bemused by their sudden wealth, and always point them towards financial advisers. The difference is, you *haven't* won the pools. This money has to secure your future.

STATE BENEFITS

Signing On

You may hate the idea of signing on, but swallow your feelings and contact your Jobcentre or unemployment office as soon as possible. You have paid your dues and you are entitled to receive unemployment pay for up to a year. Claims can't necessarily be backdated, so the earlier you do it the more money you are likely to get. Don't forget to take your P45.

Claiming Your Dues

The regulations for the different kinds of benefits are a maze. New Client Advisers at the Jobcentre will look at your circumstances, tell you what benefits you can get and explain how you can claim them. You'll probably need to bring a long list of information to help them work out your entitlements: details of how much your income already is including any benefits you are claiming, your rent or mortgage repayments (written statements), your Council tax, details of your savings, your dependants and their income or savings and the details of anyone else in your household. You may wish to get copies of leaflets ID1 and NI12 for your own reference; they tell you about Income Support and unemployment benefits.

'Nobody can pretend that all this is a fun way to spend your time,' says engineer Phil Purvis, who lost his job at 55. *'Put it this way: I'd rather have been on holiday in Bermuda. But the Client Adviser helped me get onto an Enterprise Allowance Scheme to start my own technical translating business. Now, a year later, I can afford to go on holiday to France. Come to think of it, perhaps I can set that off against tax . . .'*

National Insurance
If you need another reason to sign on, remember that your National Insurance contributions, which entitle you to the state pension, will be paid for when you're signing on. This can make it worthwhile even if you aren't due any other benefits.

Sickness Benefit
If you're ill, claim sickness benefit. Sick time doesn't

count towards the one year period in which you can claim unemployment benefit after losing your job.

Freelance Work

You can do up to two consecutive weeks of freelance work without having the trouble of signing off and reregistering. *'My bits of freelance work pay me between £250 and £500 a week,'* says Rosie, an architect. *'I don't get my £43 unemployment benefit if I'm working, of course, but the extra money makes a difference because I didn't have layoff pay or savings to cushion me.'*

If you are receiving housing benefit you will know that the system is very slow to get started, and reregistering will also take time.

Free Helpline

If you are puzzled by any of the regulations (and who wouldn't be?) the Department of Employment free helpline number is 0800 848489 and the DSS's free helpline is on 0800 666555. Both run Monday–Friday 9 a.m. to 5 p.m. Make yourself comfortable while you're waiting for an answer.

STATE REDUNDANCY PAYMENTS

Many employers give lump sums as redundancy compensation and these are usually much more generous than the state scheme. You can't get the state payments as well as a lump sum.

FINANCIAL MATTERS

If you have worked over 16 hours a week for the same employer for two years (or over 8 hours a week for 5 years) and are over 20 years old, you will probably be eligible for a statutory redundancy payment. Your employer is obliged to pay, but if they are unable to – probably due to liquidation – the state will pay.

From March 1992 the maximum 'week's pay' allowable is £205, and the limit on the statutory guarantee payment payable to employees is £14.10 per day.

A Present From The Taxman

If your income went down part way through a tax year, you're probably due for a rebate from the taxman. Normally you'd get it at the end of the year or when you start another job, but your tax office may be persuaded to let you have some of it if you convince them that you're suffering from 'hardship'. The leaflet *Income Tax and the Unemployed* (IR41) has the details: your taxman will send you a copy.

Concessions For Unemployed People

Most councils also offer concessions to unemployed people, so check what is available in your area. Such benefits don't put much cash in your pocket, but at the very least, free entry to the council sports or arts centres offer the chance to keep physically and mentally healthy – a good idea when life seems tough. (See also Chapter 8.)

BALANCING THE BUDGET

If you've followed the adivce in the previous chapters, you should have a reasonable idea of how much money you have got to live on right now. Possibly you'll have some from state benefits, and some income from investing a lump sum compensation. It can never be too soon to sort out your financial affairs, so now is the time to draw up your own budget.

Assets

First, find out how much you have on the credit side. Draw up three sections. In Section A, list your income from all sources. (Don't forget this could include redundancy insurance on mortgage, credit cards, etc.) In Section B, list reasonably easily-realised assets – for instance, money saved in an instant access account or perhaps tied up in a second car. In Section C, list hard-to-realise assets, like your house.

Outgoings

Next, list all the monthly outgoings you had before you lost your job, divided into 'Essentials' and 'Non-Essentials'. A typical kind of list follows. Set out each item as shown, and put what it costs you per month now in the first column 'I Am Paying Now'.

Then look at how much income you are going to

have, and work out how much you can afford to pay. Put that in the 'I Can Afford To Pay' column. Take your time over this. You should be thinking about what the most important things to spend your money on are, because you won't have enough for everything. Obviously, most of your money should go on things that you have labelled Essential.

EXAMPLE BUDGET SHEET

ESSENTIALS

Item	I Am Paying Now	I Can Afford To Pay
Mortgage/rent,		
Council tax,		
Water rates,		
Gas,		
Electricity,		
Food,		
Phone,		
House & contents,		
Insurance,		
Basic clothing,		
Shoes,		
Car maintenance,		
Car insurance,		
Petrol,		
Minimum credit card payments,		
Professional dues,		
N.I. contributions (if not credited),		
Life insurance.		

REDUNDANCY

Your 'Non-Essentials' list might include – Health insurance, Cleaning help, Child care, School fees, Charitable donations, Holidays, Entertainment, Regular savings plans (though watch for surrender penalties), PEPs and Investments.

Essential Or Not?
Your idea of essentials and non-essentials is probably a little different from the above. A keen dressmaker may be able to adapt older clothes. A city bachelor might find he can manage without his car. A family whose child is facing exams might try to keep up school fees for a while.

Know Where You Stand
If you think you'll have to use savings to cover your essentials, estimate how long they will last before you'll settle for a less than perfect job just to pay the bills. You'll probably have many months in hand, but knowing where you stand helps. You may not need to touch any of your hard-to-realise assets . . . although for some people, moving into a cheaper house might actually be a reasonable option.

See You Later, Decorator
It all sounds quite easy when it's written down, but if you haven't been used to economising you'll find it

requires mental adjustment even to make out a budget. *'I truly thought I was being thrifty by choosing cheap dishes on the menu and getting just my lounge redecorated,'* says Karen Miller, an advertising executive who now has another job. *'It took me a while to realise that real thrift meant not eating at restaurants or having decorators in at all.'*

Debit Detective

While you have your bank statements out, check what regular payments you have been making during the last year. You could find that some relate to things you have forgotten about. Lucy, a theatre designer, was amazed to realise that she was apparently paying a standing order to a charity which had ceased to exist several years previously. *'Well, I always wondered how my bank made its money,'* she observed wryly.

Play Your Cards Right

An adviser will most likely suggest that you pay off credit card debts with part of your lump sum. While you're about it, get rid of the cards too. Apart from the fact that most of them charge an annual fee, credit cards also charge usurious rates of interest.

'The trouble is that cards are so easy to use. It's as if they're not real money at all,' mused Vivien, a legal executive who thought that she could defy the financial reality of unemployment by flashing her cards around. After running up bills of £3,000 (painfully paid off

when she got another job), Vivien found salvation through her scissors – she cut her cards up.

Overdrafts and other loans are often expensive to run, too. If you have any, decide whether you can possibly afford to pay them off, but be sure to check there aren't any early redemption penalties.

Chapter Four

YOUR REDUNDANCY PAYOFF AND PENSION

Get Advice. Lump Sum. Savings – Keeping Afloat. Mortgage And Debts. Your Pension.

GET ADVICE

If you anticipate getting a redundancy payment of some size, then it is very important to get proper financial advice.

The Early Bird Gets Most Money

If you haven't yet been made redundant but are fairly sure you will be, get financial advice NOW before the final settlement is agreed, especially if the lump sum is likely to be over £30,000 and therefore big enough to be taxed. Certain things are best done before you leave your employment. A good financial adviser will save you more than the cost of his or her fee.

Beware – Sharks!

With the rise in unemployment, a new breed of sharks has surfaced on the financial scene. They specialise in redundant people and their aim is to sell poor value pension products. If you are approached by anyone calling themselves a financial adviser and offering you a pension scheme, it is specially important to check on their credentials, however plausible they seem and however good the deal they appear to be offering.

Financial Advisers: Fee Or 'Free'?

There are two types of financial adviser. Independent advisers negotiate a fee up front, and should give unbiased recommendations from the entire marketplace. If they earn any commission on the scheme which you choose, they should deduct it from your bill. The other types charge you nothing directly, but make their money from the commission they earn on products sold to clients. The advice may well be honest, and they are by no means all 'sharks', but they will understandably be keener to recommend high commission products.

Legally an adviser must make it clear from the start which camp he falls into. Independent advisers belong to one of a number of self regulating organisations, of which the best known are probably FIMBRA and LAUTRO. All independent advisers should be registered – they should display a blue and white logo and you can check their authorisation by phoning the Securities and Investments Board on 071 929 3652.

Most financial advisers will offer a free initial

consultation. From this you should be able to assess how useful they will be.

LUMP SUM

The first £30,000 of a lump sum payment is not taxable. However, if you have received an outplacement package you may find that the value of this is taxable.

Eluding The Taxman

If you are close to retirement, and your redundancy lump sum is over the tax free limit (£30,000), consider getting your employer to top up your company pension to the statutory limit. Only your employer can do this – you can't. The additional contributions reduce the amount you receive but avoid income tax of up to 40%. You will need to balance this against the fact that you won't see any benefit until you retire. Any money in a pension is tied up, until you're at least 50.

Pay Off The Mortgage?

The same goes for paying off the mortgage. It can be tempting to get rid of it with your lump sum but if you need access to your savings later it will be difficult if they are tied up in the house. If you need to go on to income support it could be affected if you have paid off the mortgage. Also, when you start working again, you could lose the advantage of tax relief on your mortgage payments.

Invest Flexibly

Don't tie up all your lump sum in anything with a low early surrender value like an endowment or National Savings Certificates. Some of your money should go into a high interest instant access savings account with a bank or building society. Postal accounts often offer the best rate. Keep an eye open for interest changes on your account; these can drop to laughable rates when you're not looking. Be prepared to move your money elsewhere if you think you'll get a better deal.

Money magazines and *The Daily Telegraph* financial pages on Saturday periodically give the best interest rate deals. You can consult them in your public library.

SAVINGS – KEEPING AFLOAT

Until you get another job, you'll no doubt want to cut down your regular unit trust or investment trust plans. They can be stopped without penalty if they aren't linked with endowments, as can many building society regular schemes.

Endowment Savings Policies

If you already have an endowment policy, try to keep it going because you won't get full value if you surrender it. All is not lost if you can't afford to continue payments. Ask the insurance company if you can miss a few: they will probably agree. You might even be able to stop paying altogether, and simply wait for the amount you have already invested to mature. This is technically known as converting to a 'paid-up' policy.

If you really need the money from your endowment, and if it has been going for more than five years, ring around firms specialising in selling second-hand endowments and compare what they think they'll get for your policy with the surrender value the insurance company is offering. Bear in mind that some companies, like Equitable Life and Norwich Union, are known to offer good surrender values. Firms which specialise in second-hand endowments include Policy Portfolio of London NW4 (Tel: 081 203 7221), Foster & Cranfield in the City (071 608 1941), Surrenda-Link of Chester (0244 31799), Beale Dobie & Co. of Maldon (0621 851133).

Mortgage Endowment Policies

See below under 'Mortgages' for more information on these.

MORTGAGE AND DEBTS

Be Honest With Your Creditors

As soon as you know that you are going to have difficulty making repayments, let your creditors know and try and work out a repayment schedule right away.

Your Good Friend The Bank Manager?

Obviously if you owe the bank money and think you will have difficulty paying it off, you must talk to them at an early stage. If you don't owe them anything, however, don't involve them unless you absolutely have to.

Despite the banks' strenuous efforts to represent themselves as the customer's friend, and the helpfulness of many individual bank managers, some people have lived to regret discussing their problems with their bank at an early stage. For example, losing an overdraft facility (pricey as overdrafts are) may not be what you want – but it may be what the bank decides you need. You need to keep as many options open as possible.

Pay It Off With The Lump Sum?

Some people pay off their mortgage with their lump sum, but this is probably not a good idea. Particularly if you think you may need to go on income support, the DSS could well decide that you've deliberately spent your savings in order to get benefit.

Unfortunately there are no hard and fast rules and it is up to individual DSS adjudicators to decide whether you will be deemed still to possess the capital because you have paid the mortgage off. It is an unpleasant situation worthy of Kafka.

The Mortgage Over Your Head

Far from paying the mortgage off, you may have problems in meeting the monthly repayments. The latest Building Societies Association figures show that between 1980 and 1991 the number of mortgages increased by just over one-third, but repossessions increased nearly 22 times.

You definitely don't want to join these latter statistics, and you have a good chance of escaping them if you follow the BSA's own general principles for dealing with mortgage arrears. A detailed free leaflet, *Assisting with Mortgage Repayments*, is available from the Council of Mortgage Lenders.

As always, you are in a better position to negotiate if you know about the options. For a start, you should be aware that there are two main types of mortgages, repayment and endowment. Dealing with arrears is slightly different for each type.

Repayment Mortgages

A repayment mortgage pays off the sum advanced by the end of the term. For the first few years it mainly pays off interest, so the sum outstanding hardly seems to reduce at all, and you wonder if it ever will. Towards the end of the loan period, the capital gets paid off and so the sum still due to the building society starts to dwindle at a magical rate.

You can usually lengthen the term of a repayment mortgage. So, for instance, if you have 20 years left you can arrange to pay your debt off over 30 years instead, which will reduce your monthly payment quite a lot. Or you may be able to switch to paying interest-only for a while.

Endowment Mortgages

Endowment mortgages build up a sum to pay off the loan at the end of the term (with, one hopes, a tidy sum of money over). Their main disadvantage is that if the policy is redeemed early, the sum raised probably won't be enough to pay off the loan. Many people with huge endowment mortgages find them a great burden if their income drops. One way out could be to see if you can change the endowment mortgage to a repayment mortgage. However, you'd then need to stop the endowment, probably losing money, as well as suspending capital payments on the new mortgage.

For both types of mortgage, the building society might be persuaded to reduce the interest rate charged for a few months. This can be linked to capitalising interest, that is, adding the arrears onto the main sum owed and paying it all off when times improve.

Your Redundancy Payoff And Pension

Don't Suffer In Silence

If you have trouble meeting your mortgage payments, the building society needs to know as soon as possible. Repossession or 'doing a flit' aren't the answer – if you leave and your home is sold for below the value of the mortgage you will be liable for the difference, and your future ability to borrow may well be compromised.

Building societies are instructed by the BSA to respond sympathetically and positively, which usually means that they'll meet the borrower personally, go through the finances and try and work out a payment plan. Some of them run helplines – details in INFO.

They Don't Want Your House Back

They really don't want to repossess your house. It is upsetting for everyone and they will probably lose money on it too. The main advantage of repossession for them is that the property then becomes what they term a 'finite loss', upon which the accountants can put a definite figure at the end of the year. Philanthropists that they are, they'd rather help you stay in your home so you can get another job and get your payments straight again. That is best for everyone.

Disasters

Some building societies, however, are not easy to deal with, and the same applies to certain loan companies and banks. If they are putting the pressure on you, then contact a debt advice service *right away*. If you think you have been unjustly treated by a building society then you may be able to get free help from the Building Societies Ombudsman. The Ombudsman can help after you have exhausted a building society's own complaints procedure and will be interested if a society has infringed your legal rights, treated you unfairly or been guilty of maladministration which results in your losing money or suffering inconvenience. You can obtain a free explanatory leaflet from the Ombudsman at the address in INFO.

Rents

If you are renting a council or private property and are feeling the strain, you may be entitled to Housing Benefit. Contact your local DSS office. (People who have been on housing benefit point out that the scheme is *'like an ocean liner – it takes a long time to get going, and is very unmanoeuvrable'*.) If there is a Housing Aid centre in your area it will advise you if you fall behind in your rent. Otherwise, contact your local housing department.

Other Debts

Most creditors will prefer to get something back – however late it is, and however slow – than have you default completely on the debt. They certainly don't want the trouble and expense of taking you to court.

It would be easy to describe a dreadful Rake's Progress of letting debts mount up, borrowing from sharks, fending off bailiffs and ending up destitute. It's comforting to think that people who end up like that don't generally start by reading books like this. Most individuals can deal with debt problems if they approach them in an orderly and honest way.

The Invaluable Citizen's Advice Bureaux

The Citizen's Advice Bureau is an excellent source of advice for debt problems. All staff are trained to offer a certain level of help with debt and redundancy problems and some CABs have special units dealing specifically with these. Unfortunately, local authority cutbacks in some areas have forced closure or curtailment on many CABs. If your local service has been seriously hit then your regional office should be able to direct you to another. (For a list of CABs see Appendix 1.)

YOUR PENSION

Your pension is one of your most valuable assets. It may even be more valuable than your house. But pensions are an extremely complex subject which certainly cannot be summarised satisfactorily in a few paragraphs. So it really is worth doing some homework on this very important topic, and taking advice. Even if you feel that your options are rather limited at the moment, you will need to be well primed for making decisions after you start working again.

Advice On Pensions

Your ex-employer's pension department may well be prepared to give you some advice, and the TUC will advise you if you are a trade unionist. There are useful books that you can buy or borrow from the library, and an excellent leaflet is available free from the National Association of Pension Funds (address in INFO). But the subject is so large and complex that all these will make more sense if you can also discuss your particular situation with an expert or a reputable independent financial adviser.

What To Do With Your Existing Pension

If you were in a pension scheme run by your employer, you may have the choice of moving that money to a personal pension plan or an S32 scheme, which is a special type of plan used to preserve contracted-out pension rights, or of taking a deferred pension. What exactly you decide to do will depend on personal factors and could involve some guesswork about what you are likely to be doing in the future. This is where a consultation with a reputable adviser will be so helpful.

Pensions And Unemployed People

While you are unemployed, you can't make regular contributions to a pension scheme. This is because unemployed people have no 'net relevant earnings' as defined by the Inland Revenue. Even if you are prepared to pay into a pension from your 'lump sum' you are not allowed to do so while you are out of work.

This situation obviously needs reform. Until reform comes, the best advice is to put worries about making contributions on the back burner for a few months while you concentrate on immediate problems, and focus on getting another job or becoming self employed as soon as possible. As soon as you have done that you will be able to make up pension contributions.

If you are still worried about your old age, there is nothing to stop you from taking out a savings scheme, but tying up your money in a long term investment is something you need to think very carefully about.

You should of course sign on for unemployment benefit because that will protect your basic state pension, which is paid in addition to any other pension you may have.

If Your Employer Went Bankrupt

Just because your employer has gone bankrupt, it does not mean you lose your pension. Pension funds should by law be kept separate from the company's own finances, but remember the Maxwell factor!

When a pension scheme is wound up (say, when your employer has gone bankrupt) the whole of your deferred pension (the amount due to you on retirement based on your contributions) must be increased in line with inflation up to 5 per cent.

Keeping Track Of Your Pension

The rules governing pensions have altered a lot in the last 20 years and if you have changed job several times you may find it difficult to keep track of your pension. If so, contact the Pensions Registry (address in INFO).

Chapter Five

COPING WITH THE FEELINGS

*A Kind Of Bereavement. The Four Stages –
Denial, Confusion, Letting Go, Coping. Physical
Symptoms. The Dented Ego. Self-Esteem. Self-
Blame. Depression. Words Matter. The Eeyore
Exercise.*

A KIND OF BEREAVEMENT

For many people, redundancy will provoke quite
compelling feelings of loss, rejection and dismay. It
has often been said that losing a job is in some ways
similar to bereavement.

Your employer may help by handling the
redundancy in a sensitive way and offering a good
severance deal, but you still need to go through the
emotions themselves and deal with them in your own
particular way. Only then will you fully put them
behind you.

Without minimising the emotions in any way, they
tend to follow a pattern. Of course, knowing that your

feelings and behaviour are typical won't stop you from being affected by them. But understanding what is happening should reassure you and remove some of the confusion as you move forward through the experience and emerge on the other side.

Emotions may happen in an orderly sequence – but more often they come and go in turmoil. Eventually you will recover your equilibrium in a process that can take anything from a few days to much longer.

THE FOUR STAGES

1. Denial

No matter how kindly the news is broken to you, it hits hard at first. The most common reaction is a feeling of numbness; a sense of denial. *'I felt as if I'd suddenly turned into a robot. I knew I was going down in the lift, leaving the building and walking up the street – but there were no thoughts in my head,'* says one computer engineer.

Some people have what sounds like a temporary blank-out: *'I found myself at home without any proper memory of how I got there,'* says Laura, an executive.

The emotional numbness can be fairly brief, or last a surprisingly long time, as Hazel, a director in a publishing house, found. *'I'd booked a holiday in New York the following week and I went on it. I felt too busy to think about losing my job; it didn't register with me till I got back,'* she says.

2. Confusion

Denial may alternate with, or lead into, a period of confusion. In this stage, you may find that you are extremely angry – with your ex-employer, with the world, with your family or with yourself. (See Chapter 6 for more about dealing with the family.)

As well as feeling angry and muddled, you may also become obsessive, going over and over the problem as if you half expect it to go away. This is a normal stage towards accepting that it *won't* go away. By examining the problem continually you are taking the first steps towards finding a solution.

Edward, who had been 36 years with the same firm, couldn't accept, even after three months, that his ex-firm no longer needed him. He spent a lot of time, he says, mulling over his situation. *'It sounds a bit silly now, but I had a nagging feeling that they simply* must *have made a mistake.*

'I'd think: "I'll ring up about it." And then I'd think: "Oh, no, that'll make me look silly." And then: "But possibly if we discussed it . . ." I decided eventually that it would embarrass everyone if I argued.' Edward obviously did the right thing in the end. His indecision was understandable, and the further he got away from the fateful day the more he realised that his phoning would not have helped.

3. Letting Go

In the third stage, you will let go of the idea that you will somehow get your job and all the features of your old life back. In this 'letting go' stage, you still may not know exactly what you're going to do, but you'll start to talk more positively to yourself and to others, and you'll begin putting together a serious plan of action.

You may still feel depressed and emotional, but you will be accepting the real situation, and beginning to look forward rather than backwards. This is real progress.

4. Coping

This is the final stage. You will finally come to terms with your sadness, anger and frustration. You'll want to move forward and get on with your life in a constructive way. Your confidence will re-emerge and you will be more willing to consider new avenues. You will start to feel enthusiastic about the new prospects unfolding before you. It is a little like being young again: you may be in a less secure situation, but you will also see some exciting opportunities.

During the various stages you may encounter some typical problems.

PHYSICAL SYMPTOMS

Various unpleasant physical symptoms may accompany your disturbed emotional feelings. They could include sleeplessness, loss of appetite, excessive tiredness, loss of sexual feeling or heightened emotions.

They are 'psychosomatic' symptoms – but don't fall into the trap of thinking that this means they're somehow not real. They are probably not the harbingers of some serious illness, but they are real, and pretending that they don't exist or that they are somehow unimportant is not how you deal with them. Get them checked out by a doctor. He can rule out anything serious and advise on how best to treat symptoms. Supplement his advice with your own common sense.

Laura developed indigestion and rib pains after her redundancy. Terrified that she might have developed heart disease, she rushed to consult the doctor. As she described her pains, he pointed out that tension was making her clench up her chest, abdomen and shoulders so hard that they could not move freely. This tired her, hurt her and gave her indigestion. She took positive steps to relax physically and mentally, and eventually, as her anger lessened, the pain vanished.

THE DENTED EGO

Michael's job was extremely specialised. *'There are probably only a few people in the world who do exactly what I did. I have absolutely no hope of finding an identical job,'* he says. After his job was 'rationalised' he went through a period of stunned inactivity. Having decided that he hated everyone else currently working in his field, Michael began to make other plans.

As he and his wife survived on her salary and a little consultancy work that came his way, they investigated the possibility of a total change of lifestyle. They decided to take out a franchise business: *'We'll get out of London and settle in the West Country. And we'll be glad to escape the whole awful rat-race.'*

Michael and his wife have researched their plan, and talk about it a great deal, but they have not yet taken any steps towards putting it into action. To an outsider, it looks as if Michael may in time start to feel less hurt and bitter and decide to seek another job in his own industry after all.

Tread Softly, For You Tread On My Feelings

You may find, like Michael, that you need to build up a defence against rejection for a while, and if you do, it is understandable. But if your future plans are designed principally to guard against further rejection, then don't forget that this sensitivity may be a passing stage. A managing director of a major firm of outplacement consultants finds that many people have very easily dented self-confidence for a while.

'It is extremely understandable. They may perhaps ring an old friend and say: "I wonder if I can come and talk to you?" And the friend will say: "I know you're looking for a job and I don't have one, so there's no point in our meeting." And the redundant person could get flattened by that."

'Or they may send off their first job application for 25 years and they get a letter back saying "We have unfortunately had applications from younger and better qualified people." And they say to themselves: "I have 25 years' experience, and the first time I try for a job I don't even get an interview.

COPING WITH THE FEELINGS

'Of course, they have to keep trying. Eventually people regain their confidence and get a sense of realism.'

SELF-ESTEEM AND SELF-BLAME

Sometimes, saying that you are 'unemployed' may provoke insensitive or embarrassing reactions from others. Part of the reason for this is that people tend to pigeonhole each other, and may be slightly 'thrown' if they can't classify you easily.

This kind of reaction is something you must learn to deal with and understand, because you cannot let it get you down. Fortunately, as unemployment is becoming more common, the social stigma attached to it is decreasing.

Don't Be Hard On Yourself
Many people's self-esteem and self-image is strongly connected with their job. It can be a shock to find yourself without that prop. Don't criticise yourself unfairly if you feel depressed. Even the most sanguine people can feel low for a while after they lose their jobs.

'It sounds better to say you're a sales executive than to say you're unemployed,' admits Terry Cox, a gregarious and normally cheerful computer salesman. *'I've changed jobs several times of my own accord, but when I was made redundant I felt so fed up that I avoided people for a bit. Sitting alone while everyone else was going out*

61

made me feel even worse. In the end, I just started going to the pub with my friends again. I thought, hell, I'll call myself a freelance. And they can just put up with me buying only one drink all evening.'

Your Fault?

Somewhere inside, you may have a niggling thought. Did you perhaps *deserve* to go? Were you, perhaps, just not good enough?

In recessionary times, it is statistically unlikely that you could have done anything to improve your chances of keeping your job. Consider some of the reasons why people are made redundant:

Mass Redundancies

If there were mass layoffs at your company or if it closed down, it is VERY UNLIKELY that you deserved to lose your job. If everyone else went, you had to go as well. If the company narrowed the scope of its operations, perhaps your job didn't fit in with their new profile. If you were among the last to join, you would almost certainly be among the first to go in across-the-board cuts. Not much to blame yourself about in any of these situations, is there? You're entitled to feel rotten in such a situation, but accept that self-blame is unrealistic and put it aside as soon as you can.

COPING WITH THE FEELINGS

Personality Clashes
There are other reasons why people lose jobs.
Personality clashes are quite common. They usually
happen when a person consistently does or says
something which annoys somebody who is more
powerful. It may be something as simple as getting in
the way of their office affair. Then it is back to the
rules of the school playground: you're getting up their
nose, so they sort you out. It is very tough and
unpleasant. But if it only happens once, and you
generally get on well with others, then it's probably
not your *fault*, and wouldn't happen in another job.

Check, of course, that you don't have grounds for
unfair dismissal. You could probably benefit by going
over what happened in your mind and working out
how you could have dealt better with the situation, in
case something similar ever happens again.

I Really Could Have Done Better
But you may suspect that you could have handled
some things better. Maybe you weren't as
conscientious as you could have been – or drank too
much – or took drugs. Perhaps you didn't work hard
enough, or rode roughshod over too many people.
Perhaps the company failed because you were in an
important position and you weren't pulling your
weight.

Blaming yourself won't help; but you should accept
responsibility for your shortcomings, and make up
your mind to avoid the same thing happening again.
Sit down and analyse what went wrong and you will

undoubtedly spot some practical things you could do in future.

The same thing applies if everyone turned on you for no apparent reason. Sometimes this happens when people are brash. Do you perhaps put your views on life very strongly and critically? Or make many jokes when nobody laughs? If so, don't feel angry or hurt now, but decide to be more careful in the future. If you have had several personality clashes with colleagues or if your staff made it plain they disliked you, try attending assertion classes to learn the most effective way of putting yourself across, or make a point of observing people who get on well with everyone. *'When I began to compare myself with others I realised I dithered all the time and kept contradicting myself,'* says Julie, a designer. *'It made some people pick on me. I am training myself to give just one opinion at a time, in a firm voice, and look people in the eye. It's been quite hard. But I don't get bullied now.'*

If your drinking caused adverse comment, ring Alcoholics Anonymous. If your work was criticised for sloppiness, it may mean you are lazy or were just not made to work conscientiously as a child and never picked up the habit. Repair the damage by setting yourself a strict job hunting routine at home and doing absolutely everything perfectly. Check and double-check (with dictionaries and reference books if necessary) until you have built up the habit of attention to detail.

Sure, it won't be easy, but you are the one with everything to gain from sorting out your problems.

COPING WITH THE FEELINGS

DEPRESSION

It's easy to be positive when things are going well, but if you are feeling down, it can be very hard.

It's understandable: losing your job is no fun. But if you want to emerge quickly from your depression, you need to develop some positive thinking skills.

Everyone's circumstances are different, but wallowing in self-blame is never the right way to approach your situation.

WORDS MATTER

Psychological studies show that the words people use to express their feelings influence what those feelings are. Expressing your situation in rational, positive terms can help you to think in a positive way. This does not condemn you to a future of radiating synthetic cheer like an American evangelist but the following exercise will assist you in thinking rationally and positively. You can do it alone or, better still, do and discuss it with a sympathetic friend or partner.

THE EEYORE EXERCISE

Write or tape a brief assessment of all the things you have to feel bad about. It will probably come out sounding like Eeyore's lament. For instance:

'People won't listen to me with respect any more

(because I have no status). People leave me out of their conversations and ignore my views (because they think I am an irrelevant nobody). People scorn me because I have no job (and am thus a failure). We will become very poor (because I have no job). My children despise me (because I can't give them what they want). I will probably not get another job (because I lost my last one, didn't I?). Or if I do, it may not be a good one (because I have shown what a failure I am by losing it). I can't handle unemployment (I have been out of work for ages and it's really getting me down).'

Now turn all those negatives into *positives*. Consider the positive statements together with the negative ones, and you will find that the truth lies somewhere in between. For example:

'People do listen to me with respect (if I have something worthwhile to say). Others don't cut me out of conversations or ignore my views (because I say interesting things and talk sense). They don't scorn me (because they don't feel that strongly about me). My children will not despise me (they'll moan about being poor, but will eventually accept it if I do. Anyway, who are they to despise me when I've given them so much already?) I'll probably get another job and if I do it will be a good one (because I had a very good job before, and have proved I can do it). I can handle unemployment (who enjoys it? But as long as I keep trying, I know another job could be just around the corner).'

You will see that by combining both the negative and positive elements you get a more balanced picture.

Finally, a word for the lucky ones.

Actually, I Was Just Going . . .

Some people don't feel at all bad about being laid off. They are usually the ones who had planned to leave anyway and were just waiting for the firm to ask for volunteers. Any feelings of regret and loss melt away like the morning dew as they set off with their redundancy payments tucked into their pockets. *'It's like winning the lottery,'* said Simon, who had worked for what he describes as a 'hateful' hotel group for ten years. *'My new life starts here.'*

Chapter Six

FAMILY LIFE MUST GO ON

Breaking The News. Family Priorities. Matters Of Status. Coping When Everything Gets Too Much. Effective Relaxation.

On the one hand, families remind you that life has more to it than work. They offer you companionship, acceptance, fun, love and affection . . . but on the other hand, they are a responsibility, especially if you are the sole breadwinner.

Only you can know the details of how best to deal with your own family in difficult times. However, there are certain situations which are typical of redundancy.

BREAKING THE NEWS

We have all heard stories about men who try not to tell their families that they have been made redundant. They go off every morning with a briefcase and sit in the library, or wander around their old haunts, sad and bereft. These are people who are not coping, and who can guess at their panic and despair?

FAMILY LIFE MUST GO ON

Pretending you're still employed when you're not, doesn't do any good. Nor does pretending that nothing has changed financially. In the end, it will be best to face up to the situation. So the golden rule is: BE HONEST with your family and with yourself.

How Your Partner Can Cope

Your partner may wonder what it is best to do and how to cope. Chapter 7 is especially for them. If possible, both of you should read and discuss it together.

How Do You Tell Your Partner?

Tell them as kindly as you can. They will be upset, of course. If you have had some warning of layoffs, you may well have discussed it already.

However much you have talked about it before, your partner is likely to be shocked when they hear the news. Especially if you are the main or only breadwinner, your partner may feel almost as 'unreal' as you did when you got the news. If there was no warning of the layoff, your partner will probably need some time to come to terms and start to think constructively about the situation.

Involve Them

Your layoff concerns your partner as well. Over the coming weeks you should discuss all the decisions that need to be made with them. Whatever you do will affect their future too.

If you are lucky enough to have a supportive partner, you will be able to start planning your future positively as soon as you are both over the initial shock. If your partner is too upset to be of help, don't waste time being angry or disappointed with them. People react in different ways to bad news, and if they obviously can't cope, you will have to bear the burden on your own for now, or perhaps approach someone else whom you feel you can talk to.

Your Children

Very young children won't understand what redundancy means. Tell them that you will be working at home for a while rather than going out to work. If they seem worried then tell them that you are taking time off to change your job.

Junior school children need to be told something of the real situation, but keep it simple and unemotional. Explain that you are out of work, will probably get another job soon, but you won't have very much money until you do.

Teenage children can understand the facts, but because of their age they are very self-absorbed and they may complain bitterly because you can't buy them what they need to impress their friends. You can't make them more mature, but point out that the situation will get back to normal more quickly if they cooperate and help.

Ask Their Advice

Don't underestimate your teenagers. Give them the straight facts, to help them understand, and ask if they have any ideas. Young people can think very creatively, and they may come up with unexpectedly good suggestions.

David lived in a large house with a big garden. Several years ago, he and his wife had partly converted an old coach house into a 'den' for their children. It took their sixteen-year-old son to point out that he and his sisters were now really too old to care much about their 'den' and would like to renovate it and rent it to students.

The teenagers made this a holiday project, painting it with half used pots of paint and furnishing it creatively with cast-offs from smalls ads or car boot sales. A second-hand sink unit, a cooker, and a couple of paraffin heaters were installed. *'The decor was weird but four students from the university seem to like it,'* says David. *'We gave them full use of our downstairs loo and shower. The kids enjoy having them and the rent money is modest but useful.'*

Family Priorities

Apart from keeping a roof over your heads and buying adequate clothes and food, every family will have different priorities. Perhaps it seems especially important to keep the pets, keep the car, have a decent Christmas for the kids and stay in contact with friends and neighbours.

As well as discussing priorities you and your partner should organise your money, in particular the daily or weekly budget that you will have to manage on from now. You may have a lump sum from your employer, but don't treat it like income; there are ways in which it will help secure your future. (See Chapter 3 on *Financial Matters*.)

Facing It Alone
If you live alone, dealing with your redundancy can be more difficult as you haven't anyone immediate to talk to. However, you don't have to shoulder the family responsibilities and guilt either. Ensure that you have a friend and/or a counsellor you can lean on.

Jobhunting
Chapter 10 deals in detail with jobhunting. Your partner can probably help you in various ways, especially if they have useful ideas or practical skills like typing. At the very least, they can help you maintain an office area in your home from which you can conduct your job hunt.

Ain't Leavin' Texas
This is not the time to be talking about big decisions. Your wish for another baby, or your desire to upgrade the car should be shelved for now. Even if you feel

perfectly calm, you will need some time to adjust and go through the emotions which accompany redundancy.

A supermarket executive and his wife spent £2,000 on a holiday 'to get away from it all', after he'd been made redundant. He now regrets it and wishes he'd saved the money. *'I was in such a funny state of mind. Quite cool and collected, but the holiday is just a blur. I can't remember it. I think I was worried about what I was going to do when I got back.'*

MATTERS OF STATUS

The sudden loss of status along with everything else can seem the most bitter blow to anyone who has held an important position, or invested a great deal of themselves in their work.

It is always possible to bite the bullet and adapt completely to the new situation. But this can be awfully hard to do. Many people prefer to keep some symbols around to remind them of the high status they hope to regain.

Keep Some Symbols?
No sane person will depart for cloud cuckoo land, pretend that it's all right to tear up the credit card bills and continue eating those cosy dinners at expensive restaurants. However, after you and your partner

have completed your financial assessment, you may discover that you can keep some luxuries. A good car, for instance, might well need less maintenance than an older one, and the road tax will be the same. Selling it will be a boon to the dealer, but won't line your pocket. If you cut down on your mileage, perhaps you can keep it? If you have a secure garage you might consider changing to a less expensive type of insurance cover – though this is of course a risk. You'll certainly minimise wear and tear and cut petrol bills by walking more.

Likewise, while you may not be able to go on shopping sprees for expensive clothes you can at least keep the ones you have looking good. Even buying decent soap and shampoo rather than the cheapest can boost your morale.

Financing Your Symbols

If you have had the chance to plan for your redundancy and have set up a special fund for this purpose it will be easier to keep a few little luxuries. Your income might be sufficient to keep a luxury going. Another way of financing it is by selling off items which you don't actually use or want.

Most homes have these: exercise bikes nobody ever exercises on, a fancy but boring garden statue, a luxury coffee machine that's too much effort to use. Put discreet small ads in local papers (or try LOOT in London – it does not charge advertisers and your phone number is all that identifies you).

A Sense of Perspective

You don't need to be told to keep a sense of perspective. As Dr Johnson pointed out, you never find anybody trying to convince you that you can live comfortably on a *substantial* income; it follows that you have to make some effort and maybe sacrifices to live comfortably on a reduced income. Nobody should end up selling the kitchen oven or falling behind on the mortgage just so they can continue to get all their food delivered from Harrods or drive a Mercedes.

COPING WHEN EVERYTHING GETS TOO MUCH

If your redundancy comes on top of other problems, you might find that things begin to get too much for a while, as they did for one ex-aircraft worker.

'I began to feel quite unlike myself. I was so angry it made me frightened. I didn't even want to be in this world. When my mum had to have an operation I got so worried about her that I couldn't seem to calm down. I'd look in the mirror and think "Is that me? No, it's just a face in the glass, I'm not like that."'

Job loss causes stress at the best of times. If it adds to some other major problem then the stress levels can soar. If you are receiving outplacement counselling your counsellor should be able to spot that you need extra help and tailor the programme to help you.

If you are coping on your own, then you will probably realise when things are getting out of hand. It will seem as if the problems keep hitting you and you can't think of what to do about them. In that case, you might need extra help to realise that there are things you *can* do.

Marriage

It would be nice to think that all partners are supportive, but sometimes they aren't. Rows escalate and life becomes tense at home. Relate, the marriage guidance service, can be helpful. It sees many couples suffering from the stresses and strains of redundancy. Look them up in your local phone book or write to the address at the end of the chapter.

The Samaritans

This telephone helpline does not just help people who feel suicidal. They are not a kind of psychological Citizen's Advice Bureau and aren't necessarily experts on social services or medical treatments, but they offer trained sympathetic listening, often come up with useful suggestions and can help you sort your ideas out. You'll find their number in your local directory.

Pride or shyness may stop you discussing your problems with friends or family, or you may be alone and have nobody to talk to. You may be able to get into useful conversations about things that are worrying you by mentioning the subject casually to others. They may pick it up in the conversation and this will offer you a dignified chance to chip in with what you need to say.

Family Life Must Go On

Face To Face Counselling
If you decide you may need counselling, and have a sympathetic doctor, ask him or her what is available in your area. With public health cutbacks, you'll probably find there isn't much free help, and access to what there is is very limited. You may have to look at private help.

Individual Or Joint?
If your problems involve relationships within the family in any way, consider family counselling – Relate can advise you. But if the problems seem to be inside your own head, individual counselling might be best. (Many counsellors offer either family or individual counselling, as needed.)

Private Help
As you will probably be on a tight budget, do consider all alternatives before opting for private therapy. It might be worth having a consultation to see if it is worth spending part of your savings to get through this rough patch.

Therapy
Therapy and counselling overlap. As human beings are a very long way from understanding how the brain works, you can be sure that no therapy has the one unique secret of scientific correctness.

Finding A Therapist

If your doctor can't suggest anyone, then ask the
British Association for Counselling for their list of
practitioners. You may be recommended a therapist
by a friend, or simply try one 'blind'. Ring them up
and ask them to explain what they do. If a therapist
doesn't make a good impression on you at once, try
someone else who does.

Don't ever consider a therapist who says that their
treatment can take months or years to be truly
successful. You could be hanging on forever.

Costs

Even if therapy is really helping, how long can you
bear the expense? The best advice is to stop as soon as
you feel you possibly can. You can always go back.

I Love My Therapist

There's a slight risk of becoming emotionally
dependent on your therapist. If you feel this is
happening, be strong and stop the therapy
immediately. Work on widening your circle of
activities and friends instead (see Chapter 8). It may be
hard, but you don't need more problems in your life at
this stage – and loving someone who charges money to
see you *is* a big problem.

Therapy helps many people but it is not magic.
After your first visit, consider whether it has actually
helped. If it hasn't, don't continue.

Religion

Confirmed agnostics will not find religion helpful, but if you are even slightly religious it might help to get involved in spiritual matters when secular life seems bleak. Your local religious community will usually offer personal support and may give you a different perspective on life.

In particular, if you are a nominal Christian and have not been to church, one of your local churches probably offers a more lively approach than you remember. The atmosphere of concern can brighten up many people when they feel 'down', especially if their families are not much help.

Even if religion does not make sense to you, your local church group will probably offer you human kindness when you need it, and this is worth a lot.

EFFECTIVE RELAXATION

If you find difficulty in relaxing, investigate classes or books and tapes which tell you how to relax.

Here is a relaxation technique which you may find helpful.

Relax

Choose a time when you won't be disturbed, and a warm spot in which to lie flat on your back in a comfortable position. Close your eyes and consciously relax your limbs in turn, then your face, neck and body muscles until you feel limp and heavy all over. While you are doing this, tell yourself quietly that you are going to deal calmly with the matter that is foremost in your mind. Breathe slowly and regularly for 30 breaths.

If this is not enough but you want to prepare yourself to tackle a problem calmly and constructively, continue as follows:

Tell yourself that you will shortly enter a relaxed yet alert state of mind from which you will be able to emerge whenever you want. In this state of mind, you will consider your problem calmly and plan an effective course of action.

Positive, Specific

Tell yourself what you are going to do using positive, specific language. For instance: 'I will keep important points clearly in my head during my interview tomorrow,' *not* 'I won't panic in my interview.' Or 'I will be friendly and dignified and make appropriate eye contact during my interview,' rather than 'I won't be shy when I have my interview.'

Having prepared your mind, tell yourself that you are going to put yourself into a deeply relaxed state by counting to ten, and that you will at any time be able to emerge from that state if you want to by counting backwards from ten to zero.

Then imagine that you are slowly floating downwards through ten layers of ground. Count off the layers, feeling yourself sinking deeper with each number. When you reach 'ten', you will feel very calm. If you don't, then 'descend' a few more levels until you feel totally relaxed.

Remind yourself that you are going to stay awake, and tell yourself calmly and briefly again what you are going to do. Remember to be *positive and specific*.

1) Lie there for a little while thinking about your problem and how you are going to handle it well.

2) When you feel satisfied you have got it fixed in your mind, tell yourself that you are going to rise up to the everyday world again after counting backwards from ten (or whatever number you got down to).

3) Then, count backwards, feeling yourself 'rising' through the layers with each number.

4) When you have reached the 'top' lie there for a while, calmly, with your eyes closed.

5) Then tell yourself that you will recite 'A,B,C,D,E' slowly, and open your eyes gradually as you say each letter, having them fully open, and being fully awake and alert by 'E'.

6) Then do it – recite up to 'E' gradually, and open your eyes and become fully alert by the time you reach 'E'.

7) Get up and have a glass of water.

If it helps, you can get someone else to talk you through the exercise. Discuss with them what you want to achieve and then let them read you the above instructions.

Chapter Seven

FOR PARTNERS

The Basic Picture. Feelings Matter. A Partner's Role. Reducing The Stress – Coping With Typical Problems. Who Else Can Help?

THE BASIC PICTURE

Shocks, Stresses And Strains

Often, coping together with the stress of redundancy strengthens a relationship. Nurses Mia and Hil both lost their jobs in the same month, but they have now decided to emigrate and are excited about their new future. *'We feel our relationship has strengthened now we have supported each other through such a bad time,'* says Mia.

Nevertheless, Relate, the relationships guidance service, does find that the number of troubled relationships increases in hard times.

'Jobless people may get very depressed and sit around not wanting to do anything,' says its spokeswoman, Zelda West Meads. *'They quarrel with their families, lose interest in sex and men even become impotent – it is not permanent, but it seems very worrying at the time. We see*

more violence, suicidal thinking, excessive drinking.
Sometimes if people have got into debt they'll try and
gamble their way out of it.'

You may feel almost as shocked as your partner does
if he or she loses their job. In fact, in some ways it is
almost harder for you than for them. However, there
are certain important things which you should do, and
encourage your partner to do too.

1. Tackle This Together

You are living together, so redundancy affects both
of you and you should both try to see it as a joint
problem. Relate recommends that couples should
encourage each other to talk about the full implications
of the situation. *'Talk about how you are both feeling,*
listen to your partner's feelings. Realise that your partner is
feeling awful, and so are you, and share it,' says Zelda
West Meads.

2. Acknowledge The Situation

It has happened. It cannot be undone. You both need
to look at the situation and see how you can turn it to
your best advantage.

3. Sort Out Money

You should get the money sorted out. Fix up debt
counselling or talk to the building society if necessary.
Sort out a budget together, and keep to it.

4. Exercise

Take regular exercise, perhaps with your partner, and encourage them to do the same.

5. Keep A Routine

Keep a routine going, and encourage your partner to do the same. If necessary, help them figure out a routine to follow. Help them to set up an office, encourage them to visit the job club. Don't let them stay in bed all day.

FEELINGS MATTER

These comments may help you to deal with some of the psychological problems that could arise if your partner becomes redundant.

Avoid Blame And Bitterness

If you are bitter about the way your partner has been treated, by all means admit it, but don't let it get out of hand. The energy you waste on bitterness would be better used in pushing you both forward to better things. If you feel especially angry with someone, say an ex-colleague of your partner's, resolve to 'get even' one day when you are in a position to. When that day comes you may not care any more; meanwhile you will have avoided wasting your energy *now* on fruitless rage.

FOR PARTNERS

Listen
Your partner may feel 'bereaved' for a while. Bereaved people need to talk about what they have lost, as part of the healing process. Sometimes it can help if you just sit back and let your partner talk about their fears and feelings.

Be Positive
However bad you feel, it won't help if you are pessimistic. The die is cast, and you and your partner must live with it. You will both feel a lot better if you can look on the bright side.

Don't Blame
It's tempting to tell your partner that they lost their job because of their bad temper, or complain that money is so hard because they are spending so much. Blaming each other will serve no purpose but to demoralise you both and cause rows.

I Need Your Love
Now that your partner is in trouble he or she needs your love and support, and you need theirs, to work through this together.

A PARTNER'S ROLE

Your partner should take the basic responsibility of looking for their new job – writing the letters, going to interviews, networking and so on. Your part is to encourage him or her to do the right things, be supportive and keep life going as normally as possible for the whole family.

Not Me?

You could find this quite hard to do. Maybe this supportive, keeping-things-going role isn't one you generally play. Maybe your partner isn't fulfilling their part of the deal, but sitting around, throwing tantrums, or picking on you instead of looking for work. Perhaps your partner is coldly shutting you out, or treating you badly. Perhaps you suspect your partner is having an affair. Ways of coping with these types of problem are detailed later in the chapter.

You Are Not A Mad Scientist

You are not your partner's creator. You can't take over their body and mind and make them feel and act differently. You can't network their contacts or make them act lovingly if they don't feel like it.

What you can be is constructive. Try to understand what your partner is feeling. Use your knowledge of the way they think, to boost them and help them feel better about themselves. Remind them of useful things they can do, and encourage them to keep doing them. Encourage them to seek work in a structured way. Keep the lines of communication open between you. If your partner is behaving badly or driving you mad, try to get them to talk about it and understand your point of view. And do all the practical things to help which you can.

Yes, it is easy to give such advice; it is not so easy to put it into practice. Some ways of lessening your burden are suggested later in this chapter.

I Never Promised You A Rose Garden

Everybody has bad times. Unless you're a real masochist and want to add a bitter breakup to all your other problems, you are stuck with your partner, and the situation, for now. You can only do your best to deal with it.

Don't Forget Love

Do not forget the most important thing of all. Even if your partner is behaving badly and everyone is miserable, if you loved them before this happened, you can love them still and love them again in the future. It will strengthen your relationship very much if you can get through this difficult time.

Focus On The Fun

There are still good things you can do together. If you

have a good sex life, enjoy that. If you like jogging together, or taking country walks, carry on. If you are both interested in your children's development, or if you like reading, or cosy evenings in front of the TV, make sure you continue with them. It's easy to let everything go if you feel bad. But you need them more than ever now.

REDUCING THE STRESS – COPING WITH TYPICAL PROBLEMS

Reduced Lifestyle

You, like your partner, must adjust to a change of lifestyle. You may dutifully economise, hate it and feel guilty for hating it. The best thing to do is to try and unload these worries on a kindly listener.

Dana, whose executive husband Ian lost his job after a merger, was tormented at the idea of losing her lifestyle. *'Our holidays, our dinner parties. It was torture. I had visions of myself trailing round the Oxfam shop for clothes. I hated myself for my materialism, but that was how I felt. Luckily my dad understood. And I can rely on him to be discreet. So I just bent his ear with my complaints.'*

Money Rows

Katy and Don argued constantly after Don was made redundant, and most of their rows were about money. Katy was extravagant, Don felt bad that he didn't earn anything. Together they drew up a budget. Katy stuck to it faithfully, although it was difficult, and Don bit back his paranoid idea that Katy despised him because he wasn't earning. He even kept his mouth shut when Katy made the occasional budgeting lapse. The rows about money stopped.

Privacy Please

Richard works from home as a writer. He values being alone in the house during the day and having his wife Jo around drove him mad. *'She thought she was being unobtrusive, but she was in and out of my study all day, asking me if I wanted coffee, or something. I tried to be patient but the poor thing had nothing to do. She's a bundle of energy and jobhunting didn't take all her time by any means.'*

Richard suggested Jo learned to swim. Jo liked the idea, and went swimming every day for two hours. Richard also set aside two separate hours in the daytime when Jo could come and talk with him if she wanted. *'She didn't always want to, but sometimes she did. She was still in my way, but putting a time limit on it helped. Thank God it didn't take her long to get another job,'* he says.

'I'm Being Picked On'

People who lose their job generally suffer a blow to their self-esteem, so they take their bad feelings out on someone else. If this happens, everything you do is criticised. Your partner makes unreasonable demands, complains endlessly and loses their temper at the slightest provocation.

They may continue doing this until they feel better inside. If the arguments and rows get too bad, then try and cool things down. Ignore the nastiness; don't take it personally – your partner probably feels as bad as they are trying to make you feel. Use whatever strategies you generally use to keep your temper – counting to ten, going for a long walk.

If you can do something unobtrusively to boost your partner's ego or keep them occupied, you may find that they feel a bit better, and don't give you quite so much trouble.

Pits Of Despair

This is one of the hardest problems to deal with. Your partner feels demoralised because there is no work, and fears, perhaps, that there never will be.

Try to get them involved in something, such as part-time voluntary work. Don't nag and don't compete. Can you get a friend to ask your partner out to do something which they would normally enjoy?

If the depression seems very bad and your partner starts talking suicidally, perhaps they'd benefit from a short course of antidepressants. Try and get them to see a doctor.

Violence

If your partner becomes violent when he or she has never been violent before, they could be more seriously depressed than you think. They may simply be inarticulate and need someone to help them sort their ideas out. Ring Relate, or urge them to ask the doctor for help. Explore ways in which they can express some of their anger and tension physically – perhaps by taking up some vigorous training.

However, if the violence becomes habitual, then you can't let it continue. Contact your doctor or law centre. If you are female your local women's centre will advise you.

'Stay Away From Me'

If your partner ignores you and brushes aside everything you say, make it clear that you are willing to talk and then leave them alone for a bit to try and deal with things in their own way. Perhaps they are afraid to face you because they feel so worried or they may simply be the type who copes better if they have some mental space to get their ideas into order.

Review the situation. It is plainly not healthy if your partner spends a fortnight sitting alone drinking, or doesn't make a single effort to find a job.

Procrastination Corner

Perhaps you have given your partner space and he or she is still sitting all day in the local cafe watching the world go by? In that case, they may be procrastinating – this is especially likely if they seem quite happy doing nothing for hours and hours.

REDUNDANCY

Inside their heads, they are making themselves feel better by pretending that everything will be fine if they offer a heart full of hope, the odd job application – and perhaps a pinch of fairy dust.

Confront them kindly but firmly with the facts (and perhaps the figures). Explain how they, you, and the children will suffer when money runs out. Ask them to tell you exactly what they are doing to improve the situation. Be prepared for some bad temper as you intrude on their rosy little paradise, but be firm till you see some action.

Sex Is No Fun Any More

Sex often goes wrong when things get tough. The trouble is nearly always temporary. The reason may be simple stress and disruption, which can play havoc with many people's sex lives. General depression and loss of self-esteem can also be a cause, or the trouble might be something specific: perhaps he is upset with her for having a job when he doesn't, so he feels like pushing her away; perhaps she is upset with his constant irritability, so can't feel loving towards him.

You should both understand that problems with sex are both temporary and widespread after redundancy. Angry or critical arguments don't help, but if you can talk about it calmly, do so: you could reassure each other and perhaps think of ways around the problem. Erotic massage and sex games without the expectation of the sex act can help get things back to normal; if you both agree NOT to have sex, then human nature is perverse enough for it to become more appealing.

FOR PARTNERS

If you are still worried after a while and matters don't improve, don't fight or sink into despair. Ask the doctor to refer you to a psychosexual therapist.

Very rarely, loss of sex drive is due to illness which coincidentally springs up. You can rule that out by having a medical checkup.

Affairs

Sometimes one partner or the other has an affair. This can be a hard blow and is a betrayal. Nobody can tell you how to react. Do consider that when people have affairs at stressful times it is usually an escape from unhappiness, rather than a brutal rejection of a partner. It is like a drug, or drink – irresponsible and generally short-term. But, weak and foolish though it is, it offers the erring individual something to think about and look forward to when the days seem full of uncertainty and anxiety. The loyal husband or wife, by contrast, shares the problems and doesn't offer any sense of escape.

That does not of course lessen the sense of betrayal which a deceived partner feels. If this has happened to you, you may just want to get out. But, if possible, consider whether it might be wiser to keep your marriage going – perhaps for reasons of security or stability – until your partner has work and other aspects of life are more normal. To add separation to redundancy might be like throwing petrol onto a dangerous fire.

If possible, talk to a clear-headed friend or an impartial counsellor, or write down your options and all their pros and cons.

REDUNDANCY

Wo/Men Are So Different . . .

Relate notes that women don't lose as much self-esteem as men do when they become redundant. Women can gain status in other ways – like being a good mother. But some men feel they are on the scrap heap if they lose their job. Their partners should understand this, be tactful and not make them feel small in any way.

Women, however, often value the money, company and independence their jobs give them. Their menfolk should not underestimate this. When Olga lost her part-time job in a flower shop, her husband Dan, a well-paid accountant, pointed out that since she hardly earned anything she should stay at home and he would give her an allowance. He thought he was being kind; Olga was humiliated. It took a major row for Dan to realise how insensitive he had been.

Drink, Drugs, Gambling

If your partner is drinking too much, taking too many drugs or gambling, try to discuss this with them. If they seem to want to stop, put them in touch with an appropriate organisation – addresses are in INFO.

If you can't persuade your partner to ask for help, or if they won't admit to having the problem, don't wear yourself out arguing with them. Ask your doctor for advice on how *you* should cope, or contact self-help organisations who will understand exactly what you are going through. They will offer emotional support and advice to families, and will tell you what help is available in your area.

WHO ELSE CAN HELP?

As well as the specialist addiction groups, other individuals and organisations may be able to help you deal with relationship and emotional problems connected with redundancy.

Relate
Relate helps with most relationship problems. They offer a preliminary meeting within a week or so, and then you go on the waiting list for any time from a few days to several months.

Doctors
If you find that this is too long to wait, try your doctor – doctors don't all have particularly good counselling skills but they can assess whether there is a clinical problem, such as depression, which requires medication. They can probably also refer you for counselling, especially if you ask.

Religious Groups
Your local church may be able to help. Some churches or religious groups are friendly and welcoming, offering human support and perhaps practical help, like occasional babysitting to allow a deeply stressed couple to have a night out. A sympathetic religious

leader may be prepared to talk to a partner who is not behaving well, and try to persuade them to be more constructive. He or she may also be able to offer dispassionate and kindly comments which may help you see your situation in a fresh light.

Friends

Sometimes friends can be of enormous help, but ensure that the person you are confiding in is trustworthy and discreet. If they normally enjoy a gossip, then they may well gossip about you behind your back. Even if they don't mean any harm, do you think you would mind?

Family

You know your family best, and can judge which, if any, members you can confide in. Do not underestimate them; they can sometimes surprise you. Judith did not want to tell her elderly mother about her husband's redundancy in case it worried her. However, when her mother found out, she was not as devastated as Judith thought she would be. In fact, she was able to give Judith many useful tips about managing on a strict budget. *'Mum had lived through some hard personal times and survived. Far from me worrying her, she reassured me,' Judith said.*

Chapter Eight

THE DEMON LETHARGY

Daily Routine. Oceans Of Time. Voluntary Work.

Fans of the blackly funny 'Simpsons' cartoons may remember the unemployed Homer slumping on the sofa, demoralised, to watch 'Loaftime'. This TV channel for the out-of-work focused on strategies for winning the lottery and was sponsored by 'Duff: The Beer That Makes The Days Fly By'.

Naturally, Homer soon surfaced from despair. But in real life, the spectre of idle days stretching ahead is often a serious problem. One of the best things you can do when you are redundant is to turn this time to good use, not just from the career point of view but for your own personal survival in the quality-of-life stakes.

'It used to infuriate me when people said, oh, lucky you, all that free time,' says Hazel, a director in a publishing firm. *'There is nothing lucky about losing your job and I'd never, ever want to be unemployed again. Still, some things I did to help myself like aerobics and cooking are now part of my life. So I'd advise anyone who loses their job to structure their days and have a go at something constructive.'*

DAILY ROUTINE

Many newly redundant people are so overcome by the whole thing at first that they just sink into lethargy. *'You get to feel you've achieved major things if you write one letter in the day and feed the cat,'* remarks Rosie, an architect.

Too much empty time can also create a feeling of panic. Every possibility in the world seems to run through your head but there is nothing you can concentrate on. A routine will help you focus on what you hope to achieve.

As well as making you more efficient, keeping to a routine will also boost your self-confidence, often an early casualty of unemployment. Josh Blyth, a supermarket manager, lost his job when his company was taken over. Freed from the need to get up early, he began lying in bed later and later. *'After two months, I was spending most of the day in bed and most of the night sitting up alone watching videos. I felt disgusting, so I got my sister to phone me every morning and make sure I got up.'*

Get Up

The first, and most obvious element of a routine is to GET UP, but this can be easier said than done. Josh's solution – to get someone else to remind you to get out of bed – is probably the best. You will find it less trouble to get up if you know the alternative is explaining why you haven't done so.

THE DEMON LETHARGY

Get Dressed
Now you are up, getting dressed is the next target. If you live with other people, especially children, you can safely hand it to them to point out deficiencies in your morning appearance. Take it. Act on it. You will feel a great deal better if you are smartly dressed and prepared to face the day.

Timetable It
Even if you dislike sticking to timetables, you must stay in the habit of working regularly. Keeping to a timetable is the best way to do this when you are unemployed. Write out exactly when you will do all the things on your target sheet and do them. Don't deviate from your timetable routine unless you find yourself filling your day with other useful activity which crops up.

Everyone's timetable will be different, but a typical one could look like this:

7.30 a.m. Get up, dressed, washed, breakfast.
8.30 a.m. Make bed, wash up, etc.
9.00 a.m. Go swimming.
10.00 a.m. Visit library. Note sits vac and check trade press re latest developments in field of work, including company closures and expansions. Make notes if necessary.
11.30 a.m. Write letters of application for jobs advertised in sits vac (if any); draft unsolicited letter to company mentioned in trade press.
1.00 p.m. Lunch.

1.30 p.m. Update and adapt CV to fit profiles of jobs you are applying for. Post applications.
2.00 p.m. Do outstanding household task, e.g. plant winter bulbs.
4.00 p.m. Tea. A spot of phone 'networking'. Shop for food, prepare evening meal.
6.00 p.m. Evening meal. Plan and write out next day's timetable.
7.00 p.m. Watch TV, meet friends, generally relax.

Targets

Set yourself targets. Consider how many letters of application or networking phone calls you can realistically make in a week. Are there little jobs that need doing in the home – broken sash cords, wobbly chair legs? Do you even have difficulty getting down to washing up or ironing? All these kinds of thing can go on your target sheet.

OCEANS OF TIME

If you are unemployed you have something which many others don't – oceans of time. This can be a major advantage. Being jobless and having no money is hard, but if you take control of your time you can make it work in many effective ways.

Updating Career Knowledge

'Redundancy can offer people time to catch up on new

developments in their field, take a course, or consider a sideways move that they may not have been ready for before,' says Lewis Rushbrook of CEPEC, a major outplacement consultancy. *'People with the will and the time can read up enough to appear sharper and better-researched at an interview than their in-work colleagues.'*

Useful Interests

Hazel, a director in a publishing firm, lost her job one December and was unemployed till the following August. *'I had lots of financial problems and I spent hours on end in the library just to keep warm,'* she says. To while away her time in the library, she began reading cookery books and gradually became interested in the idea of learning to cook healthy, inexpensive food. *'I had the time to experiment and soon I could cook some really nice dishes. I asked friends around to eat with me and it was really fun – even now I've got another job, I still like to do it,'* she says.

You will have the opportunity to spend some time acquiring skills which you would like to have. If you don't have the equipment, imagine you are a youngster again. You would surely have improvised, bought second-hand, or borrowed equipment until you got the money to buy the proper stuff. You can do so again.

Physical Activity

If you've got time on your side and you basically like sport, get back into shape. If you are not particularly keen on physical exercise, you will still find that some kind of activity – swimming or taking a walk – will make you feel better both physically and emotionally. Most local authorities offer unemployed people cheap or even free use of the authority sports facilities and leisure centres. You can save on transport by buying a second-hand bike or perhaps borrowing a friend's bike.

If you are keen on games that need equipment, like tennis, you will no doubt have the sports gear but not be able to afford the club fees. Some sports governing bodies are making their sports more accessible to unemployed people by setting up low-cost opportunities to play throughout the country. Ask your local sports council if there are any in your area.

Things Of The Mind

You may have hankered to write, compose or read the complete works of Dickens. They all take some effort, so rather than plunging in head-first you may find it easier to schedule periods into your timetable, at least at first.

Some councils offer residents discounts or free entry to leisure or cultural events; your library will have details of any schemes in your area.

Ogden Nash wrote: 'I would live all my life in nonchalance and insouciance, Were it not for making a living, which is rather a nousiance.' You won't sympathise until you have got another job, but if you can, use your free time to do some interesting things, anyway.

THE DEMON LETHARGY

VOLUNTARY WORK

However miserable you feel, there are always others worse off. That idea probably doesn't impress you very much, but there is some cheer in helping others in a worse situation and you will almost certainly gain some interesting insights. At best, you could even advance your career by doing voluntary work.

Stephen, a building society manager, had been edged into early retirement. He now helps with the Duke of Edinburgh Award schemes and works long hours with mentally handicapped youngsters. *'I can't say the work appeals to me in every way, but it is really good for me. I have to be kindly, patient and cheerful all the time, which I'm not by nature. It is the kind of continual, human challenge that I need, and which I never got at the building society. If I didn't do it I'd probably turn into a cantankerous monster,'* he says.

When Lucy, an artist, became unemployed, she devoted some of her spare time to helping with fundraising in the head office of a national charity. When a job came up in the charity's publications department, she was offered it. She has now been working there for several years and, though formally unqualified, has become an authority in the field.

Josh did not enjoy his voluntary work at the time, but is glad he did it. *'I called at the local volunteer bureau and said I'd help anyone who needed me two days a week so long as I could take time off for interviews,'* he recalls. *'Out of their list of possibilities, I chose to work with physically handicapped kids. I didn't enjoy it much, but they needed me and expected me to turn up, and it made me feel better about myself.'*

Josh stopped helping at the centre when he got another job, but he now donates regularly from his salary to charity, because, he explains, *'Working with the handicapped kids opened my eyes to some of the problems in the world.'*

Update Your Skills

Potential employers are, of course, always impressed by people who have taken the trouble to research the company thoroughly before seeking a job in it. If you are in a professional job, now is the time to read through the journals you've missed.

Most industries are developing so quickly that workers need to keep their skills up to date. In order to maintain your employability you may need to do the same. Contact your union or professional association to see what courses are available and to check whether you can get any financial help towards the costs.

Learn to use a computer and word processor, if you can't already. This will be useful in most jobs. So will learning to type – if you are very disciplined, teach yourself from a book.

Skill Swop

If you can't afford further training, consider offering some of your professional or hobby skills in exchange for tuition. Pete, a carpenter, gave woodwork lessons in exchange for computer training. He also started a Spanish/English conversational group in order to brush up on his Spanish, and made new friends in doing so. He was all set to begin a local skill-swopping group when he got another job.

You can advertise free in certain classified papers. Your library or supermarket may also have a free 'neighbourhood board' for small ads.

Benefit Trap

If you are receiving unemployment benefit you must be 'available for work', which rules out regular commitments. This should not cause you problems when doing voluntary work so long as you can stop immediately if a job or interview turned up (and, of course, you must also show you are not being paid).

Such is the fiendish brilliance of the system, however, that you will have more serious problems if you take a course during the day, because this too will mean you are not 'available for work'.

Far be it from anyone to suggest that you keep anything from the bureaucrats at the job centre. The Department of Employment employs people to check up that you are not signing on and working at the same time, thus defrauding the system. If you are not earning extra money, and are merely trying to make yourself more employable, most people would not consider you are doing anything wrong. The simplest thing is undoubtedly to confine your formal learning to evenings and weekends in order to avoid the benefit trap.

Don't forget that you can also 'drop out' of the benefit system for up to two weeks. You will not receive benefit, of course, but nor will you have to be 'available for work'. The advantage of this is that at the end of the two weeks you won't have to go through the rigmarole of signing on again.

Chapter Nine

WHERE DO I GO FROM HERE?

Outplacement. Do-It-Yourself. Other Consultancies. Department Of Employment. Job Clubs And Help From Your Peers. Books And Other Materials. Take A Quick Look At Yourself.

'*I'd never have thought of taking two part-time jobs, but it works out well,*' says Hazel, who runs the offices for two small publishers. '*I have two phones and two sets of paperwork, and I love the feeling of being on my toes.*'

New Opportunities

Redundancy gives you the chance to take stock, even change direction. Starting a completely different kind of job will mean competing with others who have years of experience, but you may decide that it is worth making the change. Updating your skills, or training for work that uses some of the skills of your last job, could be an excellent idea, especially as employers' needs are changing so quickly now. Or you may relocate – to a city if you've lived in the country, perhaps. You might even emigrate.

REDUNDANCY

Whatever you decide to do, you will find there are now many opportunities which weren't available when you left school or college. In particular, it is now much easier to get a training – even up to degree level – if you don't have the relevant exams (see Chapter 11 for more information on retraining).

Help

You'll come across many sources of help in your search for new directions. Some, like outplacement consultancies, can be highly effective, but are expensive. Others, like manuals that you borrow from the library, cost nothing, but you will need motivation to work through them alone.

OUTPLACEMENT

Outplacement consultancies offer highly-structured and comprehensive programmes to help people develop the skills which they need in order to get another job. They also offer support during the jobhunting period.

They originally worked only with highflying executives, but more recently have begun helping lower-grade executives and white-collar workers too.

Outplacement consultants can't match your own commitment to your future, but they can offer you structured encouragement during your search for another job. Clients of the best consultancies almost

always get jobs, even if it takes them a few months to
do so.

What Does Outplacement Offer?
Consultancies come in all sizes, and their facilities and
services vary. Typically, they might offer some or all
of: office and secretarial help, career, financial and
emotional counselling, help with negotiating severance
packages, personal and career assessment, job search
techniques and strategies, advice on CVs, interviews
and evaluation of job offers.

Paying For Outplacement
Outplacement fees are generally paid by employers as
part of a severance package. (This benefit may be
taxable – check with your financial adviser if you have
a fairly large lump sum payoff.) Sometimes an
employer will let the employee choose which
outplacement firm to use.

If you pay for yourself, the cost of a full course will
probably run into several thousand pounds, and for
most people this isn't practicable. However, you might
well be able to buy as much outplacement as you need.

DO-IT-YOURSELF

If your company doesn't offer to pay for outplacement,

and you can't afford to pay for a whole course yourself, put together your own 'package'. It can be extremely effective.

Nobody Cares Like You Care

Going it alone has a major advantage: you'll never be able to hire anyone whose commitment matches yours. 'If you want a thing done well, do it yourself,' is not just a truism. In this case, it is the truth.

YOU are the person who can best recognise the job for you. YOU know what you'll accept and what you won't accept. YOU won't go home at the weekend and forget all about your job-search, like a counsellor will. YOU'll be on the lookout 24 hours a day for the very, very best deal you can get. DIY may not be as comfortable as outplacement. But if you get the right advice and support it can be just as effective, and an awful lot cheaper.

Hired Help

If you live near London, or have somewhere to stay in the London area, you will probably find it is easiest to hire outplacement consultants for a short period of time, to help you with certain parts of your DIY package. This is what one senior executive did. When he decided to move jobs, he didn't have unlimited funds, so he approached an outplacement company and bought as much of their service as he felt he needed and could afford.

Self-Selection

'Most people will find they don't need absolutely everything that outplacement consultants offer: secretarial help, for instance, or office facilities,' he explains.

'My problem was that I kept applying for jobs but didn't get interviews. I couldn't work out what I was doing wrong and needed help to sort it out. The outplacement company worked on that with me and we sorted it out together.'

If you would like to hire some outplacement help, the first thing to do is decide what you need most help and support to do. It might be presenting yourself to the best advantage. It could be interview technique or writing a really effective letter. When you have decided, approach some of the smaller companies – they are often more flexible than larger ones when dealing with individuals, and may be willing to agree to negotiate an hourly rate. Get company names from the IPM (address in info).

OTHER CONSULTANCIES

Career Counsellors

Outplacement consultants often offer vocational guidance – or career counselling as it is now more commonly called – but some companies specialise in it entirely.

As its name implies, career counselling will help you to develop your career in a way best suited to your aptitudes. If you already know exactly what you want to do, you won't need it. Use it if you want a change of direction, or if your line of work is out of date or no longer in demand.

Don't confuse career counsellors with employment agencies.

What Happens In Career Counselling?

Typically, you will be run through a battery of psychological tests and interviews to draw out your interests and aptitudes. These will then be compared with the requirements of various lines of work.

Career counsellors aren't experts on every industry, and they aren't employment agencies, so don't expect them to know details of current job vacancies.

Good ones try to help their clients to understand themselves and develop strategies for changing careers. *'We don't push them through masses of tests, then hand them a slip of paper with their future career on it, like a seaside fortune-telling machine,'* says one consultant. *'Our clients will, we hope, leave us with a better knowledge of themselves and their valuable abilities, to enable them to develop their careers more effectively.'*

Cost Of Career Counselling

Career counselling costs from around £200 upwards. Get a list of companies from the British Psychological Association (phone number in INFO). When choosing a company ask exactly what the programme involves, and check all the counsellors' qualifications.

WHERE DO I GO FROM HERE?

Employment Agencies
Employment agencies get paid for slotting people into jobs. They offer technical, supervisory and middle management work. Some agencies that specialise in sales, the law, computers, etc can be useful at higher levels too. However, top post are rarely their forte.

Their loyalty is to the person who pays them – almost always the employer. When times are hard they have been known to advertise vacancies for wonderful jobs which have mysteriously disappeared when you ring up. However, that is no reason not to try them. After all, they are not charging you anything, and they might come up with a job for you.

DEPARTMENT OF EMPLOYMENT

The Department of Employment now provides quite a good service for unemployed people. You can get full details by asking for their new edition of the *Just the Job* booklet at your job centre.

Job Review Service
There is a job review service which provides practical guidance and a back-to-work plan if you have been out of work for three months. In practice, you had better use it in order to convince the DSS that you are genuinely seeking work.

The counsellors can help you get your thoughts in order and set out a practical course of action, and they can be particularly useful if you are feeling lethargic and demoralised. But as one architect found, they are not experts in any particular field.

'I know most of the firms in London doing my kind of work, and often get odd jobs by personal contact. But the girl at the job centre suggested I sent my CV off to ten firms a week. It was crazy. Apart from the fact it costs money to get ten CVs laser-printed on good paper and sent first class, it did not do my reputation any good when my CV arrived unsolicited with lots of others – I know they just get chucked in the bin.

'When I explained the problem to the girl at the job centre, she agreed that she hadn't given me appropriate advice. She agreed that I should stop sending unsolicited CVs out, and start being much more selective. She *had* needed me *to bring the matter up; so speak up if you have doubts about what they are asking you to do. You know your field better than they do.'*

Job Search Seminars
These offer two days of help on the best ways to search out and apply for jobs, and are aimed primarily at unskilled and semi-skilled workers. They help with techniques for searching out and applying for jobs and give advice about attending interviews. There's also the chance to 'drop in' for further advice up to four weeks after the seminar.

Job Review Workshops
These are aimed basically at professional people. A computerised guidance system is normally used to

select jobs which suit clients, and they also get the chance to research more deeply into jobs which interest them.

Both seminars and workshops are available to people who have been out of work for at least three months. Clients' fares to and from the seminar will be paid, and their benefits won't be affected.

If you are eligible, do consider attending these, especially if you are jobhunting without support. As well as the practical advice they offer, they also give you the chance to talk with others in your situation.

They also help you extend your 'network'. People in the same boat usually try to help each other to some extent, and may have some very useful suggestions, contacts and personal interview experiences.

Nick, a graphic artist, got talking to a fellow workshop participant who was a production engineer. The engineer's wife had her own business, and was able to offer Nick some freelance work.

Job Interview Guarantee

Aimed mainly at non-professionals, this gives you the chance to work for a few weeks with an employer and guarantees you a job interview at the end. It is not offered at all job centres, and is only available if you have been jobless for over six months.

Restart

This is another 'you'd-better-do-it' opportunity which you go to after six months. The staff help you take a fresh look at your situation and they will offer you whatever opportunities and suggestions they can.

JOB CLUBS AND HELP FROM YOUR PEERS

Job clubs have been springing up all over the place. The Department of Employment runs them, and so do many professional bodies, trade unions and some large employers who are making many people redundant.

They are nearly always entirely free of charge. They offer roughly similar things: an office with secretarial help, fax and phones, reference material such as books and newspapers, and some advice on general matters including writing CVs and presenting yourself for interviews.

They can also offer that most valuable of experiences, a sense of solidarity and community, a place in the world. '*I appreciate having somewhere to come in to,*' explains Pete, an account executive.

Employment Department Job Clubs
If you have not worked for six months, you become eligible to join an Employment Department Job Club. By that time, you may be feeling quite demoralised if there are no jobs on the horizon. Joining the job club will be one of the best things you could do. It will offer a fresh perspective on your problems, give you

somewhere to go, help with expenses – stamps,
phones, stationery – and the staff may come up with
some useful suggestions – they also sometimes know
about unadvertised jobs.

Help From Your Peers

Many industries and trade and professional bodies try
to give unemployed members some help. As the help is
voluntary, it can be arbitrary: certain professions, like
architects and solicitors, have been badly hit in recent
years but their professional bodies are not especially
helpful, at present, to members who lose their jobs.
On the other hand, accountants and advertising people
can offer some splendid help to their redundant
colleagues.

The kind of help offered varies. It could be almost
like an outplacement service, or just a telephone
helpline and 'shoulder to cry on'. A good thing about
this kind of colleague-based help is that its approach,
and the attitudes of the people running it, will be
familiar to you. For example, the advertising
industry's benevolent society, NABS, has a glossy
newsletter whose competitions give decidedly
glamorous prizes. A night at the theatre could be just
what you need if you're broke. (In fact, from the
newsletter, you'd almost think that unemployment
was fun . . . but then, they *are* ad men.)

There are too many colleague-based schemes to
cover here in detail. The best advice is: if you are a
member of any professional body, trade association or
union, contact them and see what they have to offer.

From the BIM to the TUC, you'll find that most of them have something.

BOOKS AND OTHER MATERIALS

Many, many books tell you how to find a job, write CVs, assess yourself, do well at interviews, etc. They are all slightly different from one another. Some of the most effective are listed in INFO, but there are also likely to be others equally – or better – suited to your needs.

Finding The Right Book
Most large towns have a big book store – a Dillons or Waterstones, perhaps – as well as smaller local bookshops and a W H Smith. Don't just go into one bookshop; try several, and browse amongst the books in their 'Business' sections. It is best to buy any title that you think will really help, because then you will have it to refer to. But if you can't afford to buy it, note the most useful looking titles, then borrow or order them from the library. (You may have to wait a few weeks if the library doesn't already have the book on its shelves, or if it has been reserved by other people.)

WHERE DO I GO FROM HERE?

Libraries

Libraries have a different selection of books from the bookshop. They also have special careers sections containing trade-produced leaflets and newspapers or Careers Office pamphlets. They have access to more expensive and very useful publications, too, like the Department of Employment's snappily entitled 'Classification of Occupations and Directory of Occupational Titles' which looks at what different kinds of jobs actually involve.

They Love To Help

Librarians are trained to help people find out information and generally seem to enjoy it, so don't be shy about asking for help. They may be able to direct you to books of interest in completely different sections of the library from the one you've been looking in.

Libraries often have books which are just out of print (and therefore unavailable at the bookseller's). But however useful a book seems, you should always check the date of publication. If it is more than a year or so old, adjust your thinking accordingly. For instance, computers didn't come into common use till the mid 1980s, but they have changed working practices enormously in industries like travel. If you're thinking of relocating, then, at time of writing, the Southeast is no longer Britain's boom area. Going abroad? Communism is dead . . . and world maps have just been redrawn again, and . . .

TAKE A QUICK LOOK AT YOURSELF

Unless you are going straight into an outplacement programme, or you know exactly what kind of job you are going to do, you may like to assess yourself before you buckle down to your jobhunting plan.

Transferable Skills

You have skills in many areas of your life which you could potentially use at work. Could you transfer some of the skills and experience which carry you through everyday life, into a job situation?

The Cycling Beekeeper

Perhaps you're a gifted cook, a kindly carer, a good host, a keen cyclist, or even a successful beekeeper! You may be able to develop this interest in a work context. A love of wildlife, for instance, won't automatically fit you for a job as a park ranger, or equip you to take a botany degree, but it will have given you ideas about how to spend all that free time that you didn't have before, and perhaps you could acquire skills which you never had before.

Harriet grew up in a city and trained as a journalist, but she developed a deep passion for gardening and for visiting famous gardens after she moved to the country. She eventually retrained as a landscape architect.

Where Do I Go From Here?

Don't Be Modest
Start by making a list of every good human
characteristic you can possibly lay claim to – accuracy,
perhaps; conscientiousness, helpfulness, loyalty.
Don't be modest – make the list as long as possible.

Then write down what you feel you do best:
delegation, organising others well, perhaps, presenting
yourself well and looking good, leading a team or
coping calmly with deadlines. Again, list everything
you can think of.

What Really Matters To You?
Next, set out the personal values which you think are
important, and which you want to feature in your life.
Do you value stability, independence, variety? Is it
important to you to work with other people, keep to a
routine, improve your environment, help others more
needy than yourself? When you have decided on all
the values that matter most to you, try to put them in a
rough order of importance. This can help you clarify
the kind of work you may NOT like, as well as
encouraging you to think about what appeals to you.

Michelle, who is half Belgian, had always wanted to
work somewhere like Disney, because she had loved
working in a children's playscheme and was very
extrovert. She couldn't wait to apply to Euro Disney,
but when she sat down and worked out what her
priorities were, she realised that the personal
relationships with the children had been what
mattered most to her. 'If I worked in Euro Disney I'd
have to look smart all the time, which I'm not good at,

and I'd never get to know any of the children,' she said.

Personal Achievements
Finally, list what you feel proud of having accomplished in your life. This could include helping a relative through a problem, decorating your home immaculately, raising money for a charity, having excellent relationships with your close family. What do these achievements say about you? Do they suggest qualities which you could use in a work situation?

Match Them Up
By now you will have a few concrete ideas of the kind of direction you want to go in. Keep them in mind; write them down if it's easier.

You are now ready to research career possibilities.

Chapter Ten

JOBSEARCHING

*Organise Your Workspace. Set Objectives.
Researching The Market. Newspaper
Advertisements. Job Centre And Recruitment
Consultants. CVs. Interviews.*

There are many challenges and rewards waiting for
you in your job search. But just as the most important
thing to do in the day is to GET UP, the most
important thing with jobhunting is to GET MOVING.

ORGANISE YOUR WORKSPACE

A Space To Call Your Own
You will need a clearly defined space to use as your
office. It can be a spare bedroom if you have one, a
corner of the least-used room in the house; anywhere
that will enable you to leave your papers and files out
and which is safe from partners, pets and children. If
you can get a telephone to your workspace, so much
the better.

REDUNDANCY

Even if you are not normally an organised person, try to be organised in your job search. It is all part of the keeping-your-life-together process.

Filing System
It sounds like a rather grand name for what might be just a few box files and folders. You don't need a filing cabinet; keeping your files strictly in order in one place is enough.

Progress Report
Your progress report enables you to keep track of how you're doing. A simple piece of card will do. Enter the headings 'Company', 'Salary', 'Job Title', 'Application Date', 'Interview', 'Outcome'. Every time you apply for a job, jot down brief details under the appropriate heading. You will be able to tell at a glance how your applications are doing.

Keep the progress report with your Notes file (see below).

Take Notes
Write up notes on all applications which get you an interview or a personal response. For each job, enter details of who you dealt with, your impressions of them, how they acted towards you, any questions which caught you out during the interview, any ways

in which you did particularly well. Study the notes in odd moments, and think about them. Can you improve on your performance?

Contacts

Use a separate section of your Notes file for your alphabetical contacts list. Note each contact's name, address, phone and fax number. Start by jotting down where you last met them and why, and any other information which you think you may find relevant, and then update as necessary. For example:

JONES, Jane. Training Officer, NFB, North Road, London NW12 8QT, Tel: 071-478 3322, Fax 071-366 1112. We were last in contact May 1992 when we discussed value of short theoretical courses for new trainees.

Spoke 14 October 1992. She seemed friendly and encouraging. Did not know of anything but she is meeting head of NFB's research department next week and will enquire about possible freelance work. She also suggested I phone Peter Wilson of TTN, using her name as introduction (see WILSON).

CHASE re freelance work, November 14

'To Do' File

Use a card index with dividers numbered with the days of the month. Each time you know you'll need to do something on a particular day, put a card note in under the relevant date. Go through the file every morning.

Company Information

An alphabetical Company Information file is a 'must'. During your library researches, note or photocopy relevant news and information about companies in your field. One advantage of being unemployed is that you will have time to build up a comprehensive picture of the current situation in your industry. The information will enable you to target companies or individuals.

You should also write to all the companies which could be of interest to you, get as much of their literature as you can, read it and file it.

'Dead' File

Some of your job applications will get no reply or else a form rejection. There is not much you can say about them in your notes. Put them in your 'dead file' in alphabetical order. Also in the 'dead file' place notes for, and details of, applications which didn't succeed.

It may be tempting to see these as failures and hurl them away, but don't. Information in them may be useful later; for instance, another job in the same company may come up for which you want to apply.

126

SET OBJECTIVES

If you plan to set up your own business or take out a franchise, get moving. Consider what you have to do, estimate how long it should take you. Write them all down. These are your objectives. You should of course take advice before committing cash and doing anything irrevocable.

Chicken Sexing Or Bust

If you are seeking another job, then the rule of thumb is that the more specialised people take longer to get jobs. Anyone who insists on being hired as a specialist chicken-sexer will wait much longer for a job than someone who is content to be a general farm worker. The same goes for top jobs. We all know that the chairmanship of ICI doesn't come up every day, and it follows that high-flying posts in all companies will be fewer than lower-status jobs.

How Long Will You Be Waiting?

Just under six months is the outplacement specialists' estimate for the time it takes the average competent executive to get another job. This figure has, surprisingly, remained fairly constant over the last ten years. This is probably because as the jobs get fewer, individuals' techniques for chasing them improve.

None of these rules of thumb is infallible. You may be a filing-clerk who is out of work for a year, or an executive who has only been unemployed for a week before the next job comes along. However, your target date will serve to inspire you. It may also serve to reassure you if you acquire a pile of rejection slips during the first three months!

What Salary?

Think about how much money you are prepared to accept. If you have followed the advice in the money chapter of this book you will have sorted out your finances and should know how long you can manage before things get tough. You'll have an idea of how your old salary relates to other salaries in your field, and stay up-to-date by keeping an eye on salaries offered in job advertisements.

Not Too High

You could look for a slight increase in your salary, but if you aim too high you might find that you are wasting your time.

And Not Too Low

As long as you are managing financially, you should not offer to accept an unrealistically low salary – that will make you look desperate. It may also make them reject you for being 'over-qualified' – a polite way of saying that they believe you'll get bored and leave them as soon as something better comes along.

The only exception to this is if the lower salary is for a job which you have always longed to do. In that case, be prepared to make out a good case for your decision. Most people would see some sense in a 58-year-old accountant taking a salary cut to do some vital financial reorganising for a favourite charity, for instance. But they might look askance at a 30-year-old physicist seeking a job as a lab technician.

Perks
Fringe benefits can add a lot to quoted salaries. Take them into account when you're doing your calculations, but remember they are usually taxed.

Researching The Market

The main ways to get jobs are:

Word of mouth (networking)
Cold canvassing
Press advertisements
The job centre and recruitment consultants

Networking
Your networking is a way of getting the news around that you are available. People are more likely to offer you a job if they know you are looking for one.

Redundancy

The Old School Tie may not rule quite as much these days, but there is no doubt that the more people you know, the more likely you are to get a job through one of them. Those working in companies in which you are interested are the best contacts, but don't scorn *anyone*; even Auntie Edna might get chatting in the vet's waiting room to someone who needs someone like you.

Don't confine your questions to a blunt 'Do you know of a job for me?' Your contacts may have all kinds of things to offer; advice, mostly – or some gossip which you can profitably follow up. They may be willing to coach you or put in a word for you to someone who can help you.

People usually quite like to help, and will understand that you are not just phoning them up to pass the time of day after being out of touch for two years. But you'll find the whole business more rewarding and enjoyable if you can summon up a genuine interest in what they have been up to. Don't forget that in difficult times, they'll probably be a little worried about their own futures, and may want to help you in the hope that you will perhaps help them sometime.

Keep Control Of Your Networking

Set yourself a target of reaching so many contacts per week. Date and write up each call in your contacts file.

If you are watching the pennies, try not to phone at expensive times. The phone rates run thus: 0800–1300 is the expensive rate. 1300–1800 is medium rate. 1800–0800 is cheap rate.

If you need to phone abroad, check when cheap rate is for the country you are calling – it may be different from the above.

Cold Canvassing

Imagine a chief executive sitting behind his desk and thinking: 'We've made an acquisition – now we need another pair of hands to balance up our management team.' A letter appears on his desk from you. It says that you have researched his organisation, you know they've made an acquisition and you are now wondering if he needs someone like you. Your experience, you believe, is relevant. Would he be interested in meeting you for fifteen minutes – perhaps for a drink, to discuss the matter further?

Obviously you are more likely to get the job than if you sent off a CV which landed on his desk with 200 others *after* the job was advertised.

Get There First

The golden rule with cold canvassing is, get there first. If you turn up and you're suitable, they won't even *need* to advertise the job.

There is no sure way of getting there first, but networking helps a lot, because every little bit of gossip is grist to your mill. Reading the trade press helps, and so does scanning the financial pages of the newspapers. Look out for mergers and takeovers, new factory openings, the introduction of a new product, a

131

large order. All these signal job opportunities for someone, and it might as well be you.

Dos and Dont's Of Cold Canvassing

DO compose your letter with care. Make it straightforward and to the point.

DO be businesslike and briefly include relevant information.

DO be concise.

DO be moderately enthusiastic about yourself and their company.

DO write to an individual by name (or write to the Chief Executive by name if you are in doubt about whom to contact).

DO make sure your letter and CV are immaculately typed and spelt.

DON'T bend the truth or exaggerate your achievements.

DON'T imply you're so desperate that you'd do anything to get their job.

DON'T be too 'hard to get' either; highly accommodating but dignified should be your line.

DON'T hint that there could possibly be any disadvantages to hiring you.

DON'T be gimmicky unless you are looking for a job in an ad or PR agency; having an application delivered by gorillagram will certainly attract attention for that zoo admin job, but do you really want to give everyone hysterics?

Sample Letters

These are just examples. But they should give you an idea of the general style and tone to adopt.

Letter No 1

Dear Mr. Bloggs,

I see that ABC Manufacturing Limited has just acquired a new software subsidiary here in Blanktown.

My six years with XYZ Limited have given me the experience and skills detailed in the enclosed CV. In particular I have three years' experience of marketing MS-DOS database products. I would now appreciate the chance to employ my knowledge and abilities in the kind of dynamic, innovative environment for which your company has a reputation.

I hope you agree that it could be mutually beneficial for us to meet.

Yours sincerely, etc.

Letter No 2

Dear Ms Brown,

My neighbour, Ann Fairweather, has told me that you are seeking an extra person for general help in your photographic business. I wonder if you would consider me for the post?

REDUNDANCY

I worked for three years in Blanktown Photos, first behind the counter and then as assistant to Mr Eric Smith, the owner.

During this time I assisted with many wedding photograph sessions and I also became familiar with all aspects of darkroom and technical operation. I was very sorry to lose my job when Mr Smith retired and the business closed down.

I believe I could turn my hand to most aspects of photographic work and so I would appreciate the opportunity of meeting you to discuss this further.

I enclose my CV and hope to hear from you soon.

Yours sincerely, etc.

A gentle follow-up call enquiring if they got your letter and whether they were interested wouldn't hurt.

NEWSPAPER ADVERTISEMENTS

Trade And Professional Journals
If you are a specialist, read your trade or professional journals first. In recessionary times companies may restrict their advertising to these in order to save money. Look through back issues too – jobs may stay open for some time.

JOBSEARCHING

National Papers
National dailies and Sunday papers advertise specific kinds of vacancies on set days of the week. For instance, if you are in the media, look in the 'Guardian' on Mondays.

Examine all the quality daily and Sunday papers in the library to see which ones you should check each week, and when.

Regional, Local And Council Papers
These are good sources of lower-paid local and part-time jobs. Driving, care work, even part-time teaching or researching, are advertised here. You could also look for work in local shops, waitressing or bar work. Some councils publish newsletters which contain full details of all council jobs. They are generally distributed through local libraries and council offices.

Application Letters
Your application should mention the advertisement, with its date and the publication in which it appeared. It should briefly but clearly state how you match what is asked for in their ad. The more ways in which you can demonstrate how you match their ad, the more likely they are to pick out your letter from the hundreds they may receive.

If you think you really could do a job but don't have the qualifications, write and say so. Your letter will stand out because of that. It could arouse their interest and they may decide to see you.

JOB CENTRE AND RECRUITMENT CONSULTANTS

Job Centre

You can walk into job centres from the street and study the jobs advertised there. Ask the staff about ones which interest you. If you don't see any that seem suitable, tell the staff what you are seeking, and ask if there are any jobs that are not on display.

Job Agencies

If you are a specialist you may find that certain employment agencies advertise in your trade journals. These are obviously the ones to try first. Make an appointment and be prepared to let the agency have your CV. They will evaluate you and register you if they think you are suitable.

Many agencies can be very helpful, but don't forget they earn their living by supplying employers. They may send out your CV to all and sundry, even to employers that have only the remotest likelihood of hiring you.

CVs

Your CV (curriculum vitae) is an important document. It tells potential employers what you have done and also shows them what kind of person you are.

CV Agencies

There are agencies which compile and supply professionally typed CVs. If you don't have access to a word processor and laser copier, or are hopeless at writing, these companies could help you to produce a better CV than you otherwise could.

However, a recent 'Which?' report showed that many professionally typed CVs contained errors. Also, employers often recognised the style and layout used by CV companies, and were not impressed. It seems that they preferred to feel that candidates had taken the trouble to do their own CVs.

Do Your Own CV

Entire books exist on writing CVs (see INFO). Here are the basic things to know:

Presentation

Get the CV neatly set out in a clear typeface and preferably printed on a laser printer. Don't handwrite it – and frankly, a dot matrix printer is almost as bad as handwriting. Use heavy, good quality A4 paper with matching envelope. White is definitely the safest colour, but cream or pale grey may stand out a little better from a pile of CVs.

Keep it simple. Fancy bindings or glossy covers make you seem as if you are trying too hard. One magazine editor still sniggers at the memory of a CV which arrived in a velvet covered case.

What It Should Contain

Heading:

CURRICULUM VITAE

Below that, set out neatly your full name, date of birth, age, home address and telephone number.

Qualifications

Your highest academic qualification, including subjects and degree classes, followed by professional qualifications and other qualifications (but only if they are relevant to the job).

Experience

In reverse chronological order (i.e. starting with the most recent), list the dates, names and locations of companies you have worked for (underline the company names), adding your job title and job description relating to each company or division.

In your job description, mention your main achievements using specific information (e.g. actual turnover figures, number of staff, etc). You should aim to convey the kind of work you did, so the reader can get an idea of what you can actually do.

Don't make this too long – just a few lines. If you need to add a longer résumé of your career, do it separately in a letter.

Other Work-Related Achievements
– for instance, if you've developed a new process or written a relevant scientific paper.

Languages And Special Skills
– indicate level of competence.

Leisure Interests
Briefly indicate your level of achievement or depth of involvement – e.g. secretary of your local art group. You need to appear well-rounded, neither a 9-to-5 person nor a bore.

Salary
Put your last salary and give details of the fringe benefits you received, and indicate that you are prepared to consider something in a similar range. Don't aim too low unless you can justify it. Don't be tempted to omit your last salary; it will give potential employers a clue as to your status and level, and if you don't give it they may think you have something to hide and reject you out of hand.

However, if there is a good reason why your last salary was lower than your status justified (perhaps because the recession held pay down) then you should explain why it was so low in your covering letter.

Referees
Give names and addresses of two referees.

Working Abroad
If you plan to work abroad you'll probably need to supply potential employers with rather more information about yourself. This is more fully covered in Chapter 11.

INTERVIEWS

There are some reassuring things to remember about interviews. Firstly, your interviewer wants you to be the right person for the job.

Secondly, you won't be dropped into your interview 'cold'. You will have the chance to prepare for the kind of questions you are likely to be asked. The better you prepare the more advantage you will have over the other candidates.

Research and Preparation
Preparation is essential – the more preparation you do, the better. So find out all you can about the organisation to which you are applying, and ask yourself at least the following questions:

JOBSEARCHING

What does the company do/make/sell?
How big is it?
Who are its customers?
What is its history?
What is its reputation like?
Is it an offshoot of another company, and if so, which one?
Does it have other divisions, and if so, what do they do?

Why Do I Want To Work There?

When you have answered these questions, consider *exactly* why you want to work for this company. It is important to set out your reasons clearly. Doing so will encourage you to consider them fully, and may throw up points which you had not considered at first. If you write your reasons down, re-read them after a couple of days and see if anything new strikes you about what you have said.

Maybe you can find someone who will listen while you explain why you want to work for the company, and who will ask you any questions or make any comments which occur to them.

David, an engineer, wanted to move from pure research into more practical engineering. His wife raised questions about dealing with subordinates, a subject of which David had little experience. David responded that though his work experience was not relevant, he had been a splendid head boy at school. This reply made his wife laugh, and David realised that he needed to think more carefully about how to phrase an answer to that question.

If you can't find anyone to help you, try writing a letter to an imaginary friend explaining why you will be ideal for the job. Or even tell your reflection in the mirror.

Candid Camera

If you have a camcorder (or are able to borrow or even hire one) it can be a trusty ally. Explain to its beady little eye why you want the job. Feel silly? Well, you'll soon stop. One of the most useful things it will do is show you your body language. Examine your performance and ask if *you* would give yourself the job based on how you look and comport yourself. If not, consider why. If you sidle into the room slyly, you may be ideal for a post as store detective, but not so good as a holiday camp host. Perhaps you avert your eyes nervously, or drum your fingers annoyingly, or fold your arms and glare unnervingly when you are really just trying to think.

If you don't have a camcorder, practising your interview technique in front of a full length mirror can help.

Questions Interviewers May Ask You

Consider the following points while you are preparing for your interview. Whatever the job, interviewers will be thinking about some or all of these:

JOBSEARCHING

1. *Will You Fit In Well?*
Are you punctual, reliable, clean? Do you dress in a way that will fit in with everyone else? In order to give the best impression, arrive on time, and dress neatly and in a way which reflects the company's image.

2. *Why Do You Think You Are Suitable For Our Particular Job?*
You should have practised talking for two minutes about your education and work experience and why you want the job. You can always expand this core of information during the interview.

3. *What About Your Last Job?*
There is little stigma attached to being made redundant in these hard economic times. Do not hedge or bend the truth, but practise beforehand what to say to give the best impression. 'You may have read about the large-scale redundancies at ABC company. I was one of the people affected by this,' is the kind of response the interviewer may expect. If your firm went under and you were a valued employee, explain this if asked, but be sure you can back your statement up with glowing references, awards, etc.

4. *How Can You Help Our Company?*
This is when your company research comes in. You should have identified areas in which you can contribute to this particular company's work. Explain what they are.

5. *What Are Your Strengths?*
Most companies seek adaptable people, with good

communication skills, who can make decisions. If you
can lay claim to these qualities, push them hard.
Whatever your skills, identify them beforehand, and
when asked, roll out and expand on your
achievements. Be specific: 'I got a company bonus for
my design work on a new widget,' is better than 'I'm a
good designer.'

6. *What Are Your Weaknesses?*
Whatever you do, don't be negative about yourself.
Take a tip from the politicians and practise presenting
your weak points as almost-strengths – though don't
tell lies or be obviously phoney, of course. If you say
'I'm sometimes accused of being over-enthusiastic, so
I try and channel my enthusiasm now,' it sounds
better than 'I'm impetuous and I do daft things when I
get carried away.'

It is important to show that though you are honest
and aware of your weaknesses, you try to turn them
into strengths and learn from mistakes.

7. *What Are Your Greatest Accomplishments?*
Facts and figures will make your accomplishments
seem more impressive. If you designed a new filing
system for your last company, estimate how much
money and time it saved. Be specific about the benefits
of what you've done. Even if your greatest
achievement amounts merely to reorganising the
coffee cupboard system in 1978, you can still say that
you did it on your own initiative to end the constant
bickering at coffee time, and that your action made the
office's working atmosphere more pleasant.

8. *How Much Do You Want To Be Paid?*
You probably know roughly how much they are
prepared to pay, but wait for your interviewer to
mention money. If s/he doesn't, and you feel you must
know, then bring it up politely if you sense the
interview is closing without the matter being raised. If
they ask you how much you want, don't set the figure
too low or too high; suggest a range of figures.

Can You Ask Intelligent Questions?
Prepare a few questions about the exact job content,
why the last person in the job left, and so on. If they
seem to expect you to ask questions, you need to have
some ready to trip off your tongue.

Do not ask things you really should know – 'Have
you been operating in this town long?' for instance.

And of course *never* say anything which implies
controversy or criticism of the company and its
products. 'Do you believe your company should be
more non-racist in future?' or 'Do you plan to give
your product a more visually attractive design?' are the
kind of questions you should definitely keep to
yourself at this stage!

Chapter Eleven

NEW HORIZONS

*Working Abroad. Working For Yourself.
Training.*

There are alternatives to seeking a full-time job in the
UK. This chapter gives a glimpse of some of them,
and may help you to see what they involve and assess
how far they might interest you.

If you intend to take up any of these options
seriously you should get full advice, and at the very
least consult one of the specialist books which goes
into the detail you will need.

WORKING ABROAD

Deciding to work abroad is sometimes an option,
especially if the economic situation seems better
overseas. You have the best chance of doing so if you
have skills which are needed in other countries and
which they cannot supply from their own population.
Medical work of most types, engineering, computing,

teaching, petrochemicals and construction can all offer good opportunities.

Making Contact

Agencies and consultants specialising in particular fields (such as nursing agencies) sometimes have temporary or permanent jobs abroad.

If agencies have nothing to suit you, a good library offers the best chance of breaking in. International trade yearbooks list the names, addresses and details of companies abroad. If you wish to work in insurance abroad, for instance, consult *The Insurance Directory and Yearbook*.

If your own trade or profession doesn't have a yearbook, the librarian can advise on other books that may be useful to you. For instance, if you want to work in a fine hotel or restaurant abroad, a Fodor's guide will offer useful information and descriptions. The *World of Learning* covers the academic scene, and the *Europa Year Book* lists many foreign institutions and media.

Consider taking a trip to the City Business Library, 1 Brewers Hall Garden, EC2V 5BX (it is off London Wall – the street is brand new and is not in many guides yet). It is open during office hours and has an excellent selection of business reference books as well as helpful, knowledgeable staff.

However, if London isn't convenient, large city libraries also have a wide selection of useful books.

147

The Press

Sometimes foreign companies advertise in trade
magazines or newspapers' special sections. Keep
checking. If you see a job advertised which is outside
your scope, it may still be worth sending a letter on
spec to the company explaining why you would like to
work for them and detailing your experience and
qualifications.

Dearest Sir, I'm Blown Away By Your Company . . .

If you speak another language and can follow that
language's press, you have an obvious advantage.
However, before you send off letters of application in a
foreign tongue, show them to a *well-educated* national
of the country you are writing to, so that they can
confirm that you can write the language as well as
you speak it. Potential employers are unlikely to be
impressed by mis-spelt or too-idiomatic letters, or ones
which do not use proper forms of address, no matter
how fluent they may be.

Chamber Of Commerce

If you want to work in a specific country, ask the
British Chamber of Commerce in that country if they
can help.

I Need You, You Need Me

If you are the enterprising type you may be able to think of ways to convince a foreign employer that they need you, even if they don't realise it themselves yet. Could they, perhaps, do with a native English speaker on their team?

Forms And Permits

If you are a British citizen you will not need a permit to work in an EC country, and you will be entitled to the same benefits as the citizens of that country. Many professions now have mutual recognition of qualifications.

Outside the EC, most countries are strict with work permits. Most like you to have one or all of the following: a definite job offer, already-arranged accommodation, relatives in the country, a certain amount of money, the ability to speak English and/or the country's own language. There are sometimes age limits too.

Many countries operate a 'points system'. Points are allocated to certain requirements and the country will only let in applicants who have more than a certain number of points. Their embassies and High Commissions in London will supply up-to-date information and tell you who currently has the best chance of getting a work permit.

Social Security

You will usually be required to join the foreign

country's social security system. Find out more by sending off to the DSS Overseas Branch for information leaflets (address in INFO). This office also has much useful information about working in other EC member states and Commonwealth countries: state the country that you are interested in.

Tax

Check with the Inland Revenue what your tax position will be. Ask for their leaflet IR20.

WORKING FOR YOURSELF

Advice on freelance work, franchising and setting up small businesses often overlaps. If you plan to set up what is accurately described as a 'small business' then you need a specialist book, as the subject is too complex to summarise usefully in just a few pages. Nonetheless, much of the following information on freelance work and franchising may be useful for you, and the book list at the end gives details of useful publications.

A. Freelancing

The new patterns of employment encourage people to set up as freelancers. Many have lost their original jobs and have returned to work for their old companies – and their old rivals – on a temporary basis.

NEW HORIZONS

Freelancing suits some people very well. They like the freedom to choose their work, and enjoy knowing that no boss is looking over their shoulder. They relish standing on their own feet and like the feeling of challenge and the sheer fun freelancing can offer.

If you do well, your earnings can be good. But if you plan to rely entirely on the income, think carefully about all the pros and cons. Many of the people who are happiest to be freelancers may only want a part-time job, perhaps because their children are growing up, or because they have taken early retirement and are 'keeping their hand in' and earning extra cash.

Julia set up as a freelance cook when her twins reached secondary school age. *'I was well-organised and people liked my stuff. For about a year there were loads of super functions. Then business fell off and never quite picked up again. After another year I'd done all I could think of to get work, but I wasn't having much luck. As my husband has a good job, I stopped professional cooking and became a part-time doctor's secretary instead. But I prefer cooking and I expect I will start up again when the economic situation looks brighter.'*

You're On Your Own

Are you psychologically suited to being a freelance? Although some freelancers go into offices, many work from home and nobody will be there to hold your hand. If you want to gossip about work, you will have to find ways of meeting other freelancers – and they might see you as a bit of a rival. There's a feast-or-famine work pattern: one week you may have more work than you can cope with, but the next week there could be nothing at all. You'll need the motivation to plough on even when you are lonely or demoralised, plus self-discipline and confidence in your own abilities.

Rejection

As a freelance you depend on the whims of buyers and cannot rely on work, so you must learn to cope with rejection. And while you must believe that if people don't want to use you, they must be mad, you should also be realistic enough to wonder too if they could possibly have a good reason for not wanting you – and whether you can do anything to improve your product or presentation.

Tough Cookie

Even if you create ethereally lovely flower arrangements, or write heartbreakingly limpid poetry for sensitive publishers, you will still need the kind of toughness that would intimidate Stormin' Norman. Britain has no effective laws to protect small enterprises from deliberate late-payers, and that will probably be one of your most serious problems.

If a company can delay paying all its invoices for a month, it will gain the interest on that money. *You* will be the one who has to extend your overdraft and pay extra interest.

You'll eventually realise this yourself, as you ring around to check where all the money owing to you is. By strange coincidence, Firm A's payments are only made monthly and unfortunately your invoice is too late for this month's payment. *And* your invoice has got lost at Firm B, *and* Firm C put your cheque in the post and is amazed it hasn't reached you, *and* Firm D doesn't seem to have received your invoice at all *and* Firm E's Mr Bones, the only one who can sign dockets, is on holiday . . .

An exaggeration? Many freelances will concede that it's only a slight one, so always confirm everything in writing and make your terms of payment clear (such as 30 days after receipt). State that there will be an extra charge for a change of mind, that you will charge a cancellation penalty, and that extra work will be done pro rata and not for free.

Talk To My Agent

You must be tough without alienating those who employ you, and that can be very hard. Depending on your line of business, you may find that it is possible to get an agent who can do it for you in return for a cut.

Plan First

If you still want to be a freelance, do some preliminary research to make sure that your product will have a market. Next, make out a business plan. It should include at least the following points:

What do you hope to achieve? What steps will you take to get there? What will your capital costs be? Will you rent somewhere, or work from home? What are the regulations? Will you become liable for commercial taxes? What will you spend on overheads, materials, equipment, distribution, packaging? How much will a good pension cost you? What about health insurance, in case you are unable to work? Do you need liability insurance? Or, if you're a consultant, professional indemnity insurance? How are you going to insure your equipment? And your car, for business use? Will you belong to a union or professional organisation? And finally: What do you hope to gain? Why is it all going to be worthwhile?

Tax And Insurance

You *must* keep tabs on these. Get a good accountant who is used to dealing with freelances in your field – ask other freelances for recommendations. A good accountant should save you money, advise on tax benefits and help you avoid possible tax problems.

Tax problems are particularly relevant at present. The Inland Revenue is extremely keen to clamp down on freelances as their numbers grow, and it is becoming narrower in its definition of what 'freelance' means. The situation is constantly developing, so you should check on the current position carefully, both with your accountant and with the tax office. This is especially important if you work for just one or two clients, because the Inland Revenue may then try to describe you as 'an employee', a decision that could cost you a lot of money.

Contracts

A way of softening the problems is to aim for contract
work; this means that you will be taken on for a
specified period of time. It can be a relief to know that
you are home and dry for whatever period of time the
contract is for. But if you do contract work, you
should, in addition to checking your situation with the
tax office, ensure that your contract is a contract FOR
service, not a contract OF service. The latter would
make you taxable under Schedule E and liable for
Class 1 National Insurance contributions, and you
certainly don't want that.

VAT

If your turnover is above a certain figure (at present
£35,000 per annum) you will be liable for VAT. You
will be legally obliged to keep records of all your sales
and purchases and must follow the procedures advised
by your accountant with accuracy and care.

Undercutting

Freelances are always advised not to undercut other
freelances, thus driving fees down and ruining the
market for the future. When times are easy, this isn't a
worry. But when times are grim it can be desperately
difficult. If only Dickens were alive to describe the
dilemma of the poor freelance debating whether to
work for near-starvation wages, or for long and unsafe
hours, or in dangerous conditions, knowing full well

that if she or he doesn't, some other desperate soul probably will.

B. Consultancies

Many redundant executives set themselves up as consultants. This can be highly rewarding if you have a special area of expertise and good contacts. Many of the comments in the 'small business' and 'freelance' sections of this book will apply.

Getting Started

Until you are fully established, most of your time will be spent pitching for business. You may find you don't get much business in the first year, and this is to be expected. Hopefully it will build up.

You will need a good brochure that spells out exactly what you can do and your particular strengths. Get it professionally designed unless you have a BA in graphics.

A contract from your ex-employer is a good way to start off, but if this is not possible, approach other close business contacts. Having completed even one project, you will then have a successful track record.

Tune In

Employers will only want you if you offer them something they cannot get in-house. The principle of 'unadvertised jobs' applies here: your chance of getting your foot in the door is much improved if you can identify a company's need at a very early stage and present them with a proposal that seems relevant and interesting. Stay tuned to developments in your field. The more you know about what potential clients are doing, the better chance you have of identifying particular needs which you can help them solve.

Roger was an acoustics specialist who had done some noise and safety work in his previous company. He knew that the law had recently changed and that some medium sized and small companies were likely to be breaking the law without fully realising it. He put together a package which he mentally entitled 'I'll solve your noise and safety problems' and he sold it very successfully to companies most at risk.

Undercut The Big Boys

You won't do yourself any favours by working for cost or below-cost fees, but you may be able to undercut certain large consultancies which have higher overheads and thus higher fees, and who may be outside the price range of smaller companies.

C. Franchises

What Is A Franchise?

A business franchise is a business which operates according to a blueprint worked out by the franchisor.

Each unit is run and owned by individuals, but they make it conform exactly to the group's image, rules and standards. 'Body Shop' and 'Little Chef' are well known franchise operations. Franchises are not the same as a chain, such as Boots the Chemist, in which branches are run from a head office.

Give And Take
The franchisor sets standards on prices, goods and services offered, and you pay them a fee and a royalty on sales. In return they offer training and support – helpful if you have no experience of running a business on your own – and of course you get the advantage of selling a product which has been thoroughly market tested, and is instantly recognisable to the public. You will probably get the benefits of bulk purchase and national advertising too.

Danger: Pyramid Selling
Don't confuse business franchising with pyramid selling. In this, the vision of great profits is dangled in front of your eager eyes in exchange for selling products (often from home) and recruiting other salespeople. You may be invited along to 'conferences' in which American-style songs and chants play a large role in making you feel the company is successful and exciting; but the goods themselves are often overpriced and hard to sell. In the end, you may find

that the only way you can make money is by enrolling other mugs into the scheme.

Assessing Your Franchisor

The British Franchise Association operates a strict code of ethical behaviour and has disciplinary procedures for those companies which fail to keep to it (address in INFO). Most big franchisors are reliable but you should not be shy to ask for facts and figures on their operation, or ask them questions until you are completely satisfied.

Questions you might care to ask are: How long have they been franchising, and how big is their operation? Can you talk to other franchisees of your choice, and will the company please give you names and addresses? And has the franchisor had legal disputes with any franchisees? If so, what are the details? Have any directors or executives of the company experienced business failures?

Investigate financial details thoroughly, and ask yourself the following questions: How much can you expect to earn? How is finance arranged and what will the repayment terms be? How much capital should you have? Will you have to buy a minimum amount of goods from the franchisor, and are there penalties if you don't? What 'extras', like advertising, will you have to pay for? Will there be additional costs to you in future? Does the company help franchisees keep in touch with one another? If so, how? Will it be easy to get support advice from them if you need it? What happens if you want or need to terminate the contract?

159

Are there restrictions on selling the business? How many franchisees have gone bust in the last five years?

You might also like to check the last five years or so to see if your potential franchisor has been in the news – your library will explain how to use the newspaper indexes.

TRAINING

Rick joined a large engineering firm as a technical trainee when he left school. He was very happy in the firm and had risen to a well-paid management post when the firm began to get into difficulties and Rick realised he might lose his job. *'Although I knew my stuff I had no qualifications, so I signed up for a professional qualification course advertised in my trade magazine. So far it is not as hard as I'd feared it might be, because I am very familiar with most of it.'*

If you want to take further training in your profession, or even train for another one, consult the trade association for the industry which interests you. You'll find addresses in the library – ask the librarian if you can't find them yourself. Trade magazines often carry information about relevant courses; they may even be able to help if you contact them.

Open Learning
Open learning courses are built around your particular needs and prepare you for employment in some areas.

Ask at your local college or university for information. Your local job centre should also be able to offer some help and information. (Also see next section on building on your qualifications.)

Training And Enterprise Councils

These are directed by local business and community leaders, and offer information and advice about training, skills updating and starting your own business. Training is open to most people aged 18–59 who have been unemployed for six months or more, and you get paid benefit plus £10 a week and discretionary help with other costs. Full details in the *Just the Job* brochure from your job centre.

Try Your Careers Office

You might feel you need an overview of a higher and further education system which seems to become more complicated every year. Your local Careers Officer will deal mainly with school leavers, and will also have an extensive knowledge of courses available. He or she will be able to put you on the right track – and some Careers Offices even have special units for advising adults.

Computer Access

The computers in large public libraries should have

access to some of the useful databases around.
ECCTIS lists all courses leading to a higher or further
education qualification. PICKUP lists short courses on
updating skills or retraining for adults. MARIS-NET
supplies information about studying by yourself or on
short courses with private training companies. TAP
details training and education opportunities in your
area. Your local job centre might also have access to
TAP.

Building On Your Existing Qualifications

Professions
If you are aiming at a professional qualification, many
professional bodies will give you credit for existing
qualifications and training. Ask the professional body
concerned.

Universities
Few now insist rigidly on specified exam passes, and
many will consider admitting people with a variety of
qualifications. In fact, some universities run
own tests to enable mature applicants to show
their potential.

The Open University
OU degrees are part-time. To get one, you need six

full credits. There are no entry requirements but many students who already have qualifications can get them credited towards their OU degree as long as they request this at the start of their degree. (Note – The OU year starts in February and it is best to apply at least a year in advance to ensure a place.) With a lot of hard work you can get an OU degree from scratch in three years.

Access Courses

These courses vary a lot and may be known by names like 'Fresh Start' or 'Preparatory' courses. They are designed for adults who don't have formal educational qualifications and can lead to taking a degree. Most are full-time or fit in with school hours. Enquire with the Registrar of your local university or college.

BTEC

BTEC is a vocational (not primarily academic) qualification that covers a wide range of subjects. Colleges that offer it are generally prepared to accept adults with practical work experience in the field, even if they don't have formal entry qualifications.

Financing Further Training

Grants are hard to come by these days, and they are getting smaller and scarcer. You may be entitled to a low interest student loan: check the current situation with your local education authority. Career Development Loans cover most of the cost of retraining. You don't need to repay anything till three months after your course ends. Call Freephone 0800 585505 for further information.

INFO – FURTHER INFORMATION

CHAPTER 1 – REDUNDANCY ON THE HORIZON?

1. 'How To Survive and Prosper in a Recession' by Peter Martin (Hutchinson Business Books, £6.99).

CHAPTER 2 – BARGAINING

1. 'How to get the Best Deal from Your Employer' by Martin Edwards (Kogan Page, £8.99). This has an informative section on redundancy and very useful detail on negotiating severance packages.

CHAPTER 3 – FINANCIAL MATTERS

1. Free Helplines:
    (a) DHSS free helpline 0800 666555;
    (b) Dept of Employment free helpline 0800 848489.

2. The TUC offers advice to trade unionists on matters relating to pensions and redundancy. TUC Headquarters, Great Russell St, London WC1B 3LS. Tel: (071) 636 4030.

CHAPTER 4 – YOUR REDUNDANCY PAYOFF AND PENSION

1. The National Association of Pension Funds has an excellent leaflet explaining pensions generally. 12–18 Grosvenor Gdns, London SW1W 0DH.
2. Pensions Registry, Occupational Pensions Board, PO Box 1NN, Newcastle upon Tyne, NE99 1NN. Tel: (091) 225 6393.
3. Pensions Ombudsman, 11 Belgrave Road, London SW1V 1RB. Tel: (071) 834 9144.
4. Council of Mortgage Lenders, 3 Savile Row, London W1X 1AF.
5. Yorkshire Building Society/Credit Action Debtline. Tel: 0800 378836.
6. Securities and Investments Board tell you whether financial advisers are authorised or not. Tel: (071) 929 3652.
7. 'Guide to Redundancy and Retirement' by Burr & Harris (Rosters/Sun Life, £6.95). Some specific detail about redundancy.
8. 'Pensions, Your Choice' by C Braithwaite (Tolley, £5.95) – a good clear book.
9. 'You and Your Pension' (Which? Guide, £8.99). A comprehensive guide.

10. Building Societies Ombudsman, 37–39 Grosvenor Gdns, SW1X 7AW. Tel: (071) 931 0044.
11. CAB Regional Offices.

CHAPTER 5 – COPING WITH THE FEELINGS

1. 'How To Change Your Life' by Antony Kidman (Kogan Page, £4.99). How to deal with common emotional problems which may otherwise hold up your progress.

CHAPTER 6 – FAMILY LIFE MUST GO ON

1. Relate – Headquarters: Herbert Grey College, Little Church Street, Rugby. Tel: (0788) 573241. Local branches are listed in local phone books.

CHAPTER 7 – FOR PARTNERS

1. Alcoholics Anonymous – Headquarters: PO Box 1, Stonebow House, York. Tel: (0904) 644026. Local branches are listed in local phone books.
2. Al-Anon (for families of alcoholics), 11 Redcliffe Gardens, London SW10. Tel: (071) 403 0888.

3. ADFAM National (for family and friends of addicts), First Floor, Chapel House, 18 Hatton Place, London EC1N 8ND. Tel: (071) 405 3923.
4. Narcotics Anonymous. Telephone only: (071) 351 6794.
5. Gamblers Anonymous, PO Box 88, London SW10 0EU, Tel: (081) 741 4181, will give advice to family and friends of sufferers, and will tell you what help is available in your area.
6. 'Survive Your Partner's Redundancy' by Joy Roberts-Holmes (Kogan Page, £4.99) is a slim book aimed at executives' wives. It is clearly written with many case histories and a good address section of particular interest to women.

Chapter 8 – The Demon Lethargy

1. Local Volunteer Bureaux can be found in your local phone book.
2. The Sports Council, 16 Upper Woburn Place, London WC1H 0QW, has addresses of sports governing bodies and regional sports councils.

Chapter 9 – Where Do I Go From Here?

1. Outplacement Consultancies:
   (a) CEPEC, 67 Jermyn Street, London SW1Y 6NY. Tel: (071) 930 0322.
   (b) GHN Limited, 16 Hanover Square,

London W1R 9AJ. Tel: (071) 493 5239.
(c) Coutts, 5–9 New Street, London EC2M 4TP.
   Tel: (071) 283 1229 and has branches in
   England, Scotland, Wales and Belgium.
(d) Cedar International, 43 Eagle Street,
   London WC1R 4AP. Tel: (071) 831 8383.
2. British Psychological Association can provide a list
of career counsellors. Tel: 0533 549568.
3. Career Counselling Services, 46 Ferry Road,
London SW13 9PW. Tel: (081) 741 0335.
4. Institute of Personnel Management, Camp Rd,
London SW19 4AU, can supply information and a
code of practice regarding outplacement companies.
Tel: (081) 946 9100.
5. 'What Color is Your Parachute?' by Richard Nelson
Bolles (10 Speed Press Inc). A famous and
entertainingly written book on how to become the
most hirable person in the universe. It is published
annually, but since updates relate mainly to American
addresses, you should manage quite well with an old
edition. Most UK libraries have it.
6. 'Build Your Own Rainbow' by Hopson & Scally
(Lifeskills Associates, price £28). It is also a workbook
for the Open University WORK CHOICES course.
This takes you step by step through deciding if and
how to change career direction. Your library may have
the book; otherwise the course pack is available from
the Open University, Walton Hall, Milton Keynes,
MK7 6AA.
7. 'The Mid Career Action Guide' by Derek and Fred
Kemp (Kogan Page, £8.99) is less detailed than the
above, but offers a chance to consider how one of
many specific occupations would suit you.

CHAPTER 10 – JOBSEARCHING

1. 'Changing Your Job After 35' by Golzen & Plumbley (Kogan Page, £7.95). This is a comprehensive book for executives – worth reading even if you are under 35.
2. '200 Letters for Jobhunters' by W S Frank (10 Speed Press). A handy American book containing sample letters which you can adapt for your own use. Order through your library.
3. 'Preparing Your Own CV' by Rebecca Corfield (Kogan Page, £4.99).

CHAPTER 11 – NEW HORIZONS

1. 'Directory of Jobs and Careers Abroad' by Alex Lipinski (Vacation Work, 9 Park End Street, Oxford. £7.95).
2. DSS Overseas Branch, Newcastle upon Tyne NE98 1YX.
3. British Franchise Association, Thames View, Newtown Road, Henley on Thames, Oxon RG9 1HG, regulates franchisors and can help answer queries you may have about franchising.
4. Open University, Walton Hall, Milton Keynes MK7 6AA.
5. Career Development Loan Free Helpline, 0800 585505.
6. 'Working for Yourself' by Geoffrey Golzen (Kogan Page, £7.99).

7. 'Mature Students' Handbook' by Rosier & Earnshaw (Trotman, £9.95).
8. 'Starting Your Own Business' (Consumers' Association, £9.99).

APPENDIX 1: CITIZENS ADVICE

Northern Ireland
Association of Citizens Advice Bureaux
11 Upper Crescent
Belfast BT7 1NT
0232 231120

NACAB London Division
136–144 City Road
London EC1V 2QN
071 251 2000

Chilterns NACAB
Raglan House
28–34 Alma Street
Luton
Bedfordshire LU1 2PL
0582 480377

East Midlands NACAB
First Floor
Blenheim Court
Huntingdon Street
Nottingham NG1 3JJ
0602 418315

Eastern NACAB
8 Wellington Mews
Wellington Street
Cambridge CB1 1HW
0223 356322

Greater Manchester and East Cheshire NACAB
MacIntosh House 2nd Floor
Shambles Square
Manchester M4 3AF
061 832 3332

Lancashire and Cumbria NACAB
St Mary's House
St Mary's Street
Preston PR1 5LL
0772 561091

Merseyside and West Cheshire NACAB
Concourse House 5th Floor
Lime Street
Liverpool L1 1NY
051 708 8762

North East NACAB
19 Enterprise House
Kingsway North
Team Valley Trading Estate
Gateshead
Tyne & Wear NE11 0SR
091 482 5522

North Wales NACAB
134b High Street
Prestatyn
Clwyd LL19 9BN
0745 856339

South East NACAB
80–82 St John's Road
Tunbridge Wells
Kent TN4 9PH
0892 539275

South Wales NACAB
Suite 3/23 Andrew's Buildings
67 Queen Street
Cardiff CF1 4AW
0222 397686

South West NACAB
Suite 5, 2nd Floor
Quintana Gate
Bartholomew Street East
Exeter EX4 3BH
0392 425517

Southern NACAB
Units 1 & 2 The Anchor
Business Centre
School Lane
Chandlers Ford
Eastleigh
Hants SO5 3TN
0703 273355

Western NACAB
14 Portland Square
2nd Floor
Bristol
Avon BS2 8ST
0272 428861

West Midlands NACAB
Norfolk House, 5th Floor
Smallbrook Queensway
Birmingham B5 4LJ
021 643 3456

Yorkshire and Humberside NACAB
5th Floor
Wade House
Merrion Centre
Leeds LS2 8LY
0532 831655

Citizens Advice Scotland
26 George Square
Edinburgh
EH8 9LD
031 667 0156

The Scottish association is a separate body from NACAB.

APPENDIX 2: EMPLOYMENT DEPARTMENT FREE LEAFLETS

Employment Department
free leaflets

The following is a list of leaflets published by the Employment Department. Though some of the more specialised titles are not stocked by local offices, most are available in small quantities, free of charge, from job centres, employment offices, unemployment benefit offices and regional offices of the Employment Department. In cases of difficulty or for bulk supplies, orders should be sent to Dept IB, ISCO5, The Paddock, Frizinghall, Bradford BD9 4HD.

GENERAL INFORMATION

Just the job
Details of the extensive range of ED employment and training programmes and business help. EMPL45

EMPLOYMENT LEGISLATION

Written statement of main terms and conditions of employment PL700

177

178

Redundancy payments PL808

Limits on payments PL827

Unjustifiable discipline by a trade union PL865

Trade union funds and accounting records PL868 (1st rev)

Trade union political funds PL868 (1st rev)

A guide to the Trade Union Act 1984 PL752

The Employment Act 1988
A guide to its industrial relations and trade union law provisions PL854

The Employment Act 1990
A guide to its industrial relations and trade union law provisions PL907

Industrial action and the law – Employees' version PL869 (1st rev)

Industrial action and the law – Employers' version PL870 (1st rev)

Fair and unfair dismissal
A guide for employers PL714

Individual rights of employees
A guide for employers PL716

Offsetting pensions against redundancy payments
A guide for employers RPL1 (1983)

Code of practice – picketing ECP(2)

Code of practice – trade union ballots on industrial action
TUBALACT

Fact sheets on employment law
A series giving basic details for employers and
employees

APPENDIX 3: FINANCIAL CHECKLIST

ON THE RUN UP

- If you are to get a payoff of more than £30,000, can the excess be paid into your pension scheme?
- Will your employer pay for financial counselling?
- Get all offers agreed at the time in writing along with full back up on pension in due course.
- Speak to your mortgage lender/bank lender and agree short-term strategy.
- Consider taking legal advice if you are not happy with negotiations.
- Check financial protection levels such as life assurance and medical insurance cover provided by your company – can you arrange to carry them over to another employer at advantageous terms?

AFTER

- Keep cash on easy access account with building society or bank. Arrange for gross interest if non-taxpayer.

- Register with unemployment benefit office and check on NI contributions, unemployment benefit, income support and tax position. Useful leaflets are IR41 (Income tax and the unemployed), IS1 (Income Support), NI12 (Unemployment Benefits).
- Pension: ask trustees for a statement showing what deferred pension they're prepared to pay, and what transfer value they have if you switch to a personal pension plan or S32 buyout. If re-employed, consider a switch to new scheme and discuss 'added years' with your new employer.
- Mortgage/debts – consider reducing or paying them off from capital. Make a detailed budget.
- Check with local town hall for council tax rebate while unemployed.
- If your employer does not provide a counselling service, make sure you take advice from an independent financial adviser. A fee paying service, with commissions offset, should ensure impartial advice.

On Re-Employment

- Re-check protection levels/pension scheme.
- Consider long-term investment if any cash is left over.